We
Are *All*
Athletes

We Are *All* Athletes

Bringing COURAGE, CONFIDENCE, *and* PEAK PERFORMANCE *into our* EVERYDAY LIVES

Mariah Burton Nelson

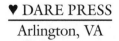
♥ DARE PRESS
Arlington, VA

We Are All Athletes
*Bringing Courage, Confidence, and
Peak Performance into our Everyday Lives*

Copyright © 2002 by Mariah Burton Nelson

This book contains some material previously published,
in different form, in the following articles and books:
"I'm Dancing as Slow as I Can" (*Women's Sports and Fitness*, June 1985);
"Tall," (*Ms.*, April 1987); "My Mother, My Rival" (*Ms.*, May 1988);
"Go Mom!" (*Living Fit*, Fall 1995 and *Sports Illustrated Online*,
February 1997); *Embracing Victory*, and *Are We Winning Yet?*

For reprint information, write to
Dare Press
2909 North 24th Street
Arlington, VA 22207

Nelson, Mariah Burton
We are all athletes: bringing courage, confidence, and peak performance
into our everyday lives / Mariah Burton Nelson — 1st Edition

Library of Congress Cataloging-in-Publication Data is available
on request.

ISBN 0-9717218-0-7

First edition
Cover design by Terry Dale
Text layout by Ad Graphics, Inc., Tulsa, OK
Printed in the United States of America

Toll-free phone orders: 888-281-5170
Author contact: www.MariahBurtonNelson.com
Or WAAA@MariahBurtonNelson.com

To Katherine

Contents

We Are All Athletes

Why We Are All Athletes
An Introduction

I am an athlete. I competed in my first swimming meet at age six; played backyard baseball with big brother Pete until Little League said "no girls"; lettered in five sports (lacrosse, field hockey, tennis, volleyball, and the best sport — basketball) in two high schools; starred as the leading scorer and rebounder on the Stanford basketball team all four years; then played in France and also in the first US women's pro basketball league, which I now think of as the L.N.E.H. — the League Nobody's Ever Heard of.

Later I played water polo in an all-men-except-Mariah league and rowed on the Potomac River. Now I play golf every chance I get, ride my bike around town, lift weights, and swim two miles most mornings, waking at 5:20 to immerse myself in that watery world where I first learned to love my long, strong body, and where I first learned to appreciate the unparalleled ecstasy of physical exertion.

Even if I awaken some day and find myself too sick or disabled to move, I'll still be an athlete. It's part of my identity, as essential and cherished as "woman" and "writer." It's an attitude that affects everything I do: how I walk, how I eat, how I rest, how I respond to invitations to try new things, how I discipline myself to sit at my desk and write, how I kid around with colleagues and friends, how I encourage any and all "teammates," how I ask for advice from "coaches," how I pursue my writing, speaking, and business goals, and how I celebrate success. It's a way of life that lifts me and carries me through each day, even those days filled with disappointments and defeats. There's something about swimming faster today than yesterday, something about summoning the nerve to do a flip off the diving board, something about rowing in perfect harmony with seven other people, that leads one to believe she is capable of anything. Everything I know about goals, discipline, teamwork, leadership, and competition, I first learned on the basketball courts, on the tennis courts, in pools and rivers and oceans.

These lessons are available to all of us.

The dictionary defines "athlete" as "one who is trained or skilled in exercises, sports, or games requiring physical strength, agility or stamina." People generally use the word to refer to those who compete in sports, and who are fairly successful at it.

I want to broaden the definition. I want us to think of "athletes" as people who make a lifelong commitment to implementing athletic essentials in everyday life. What matters in this context is not so much physical strength, agility, or stamina, but an athletic mentality: emotional strength, agility, and stamina. The "exercises, sports, and games" might be traditional ones: badminton, triathlon, hockey, scuba diving, surfing, volleyball. Or they might be the kinds of exercises, sports, and games that take place on a construction site, in a realtor's office, in a nursing home, in a law firm, or on Wall Street. By my definition, regardless of how physically fit you are, and regardless of what kinds of sports or games you play or don't play, you're an athlete if you apply athletic essentials to your life.

> We are who we are because of the stories we tell ourselves about ourselves.
>
> — Tom Spanbauer

Really? Doesn't an "athlete" need to actually *play sports*? Can you be an athlete and also a couch potato?

Here's the beauty of this proposition: If you think of yourself as an athlete, you begin to have experiences that reinforce that identity. "We are who we are because of the stories we tell ourselves about ourselves," wrote Tom Spanbauer in *The Man Who Fell in Love with the Moon*. If you tell yourself an "I am a klutz" story, for instance, you'll keep bumping into things. No surprise there.

If, on the other hand, you're willing to declare "I am an athlete," even for a little while, you'll notice a change in how you see the world and how you move through it. You'll start feeling excited, rather than scared, when someone challenges you to a contest. You'll understand that no one wins all the time, and that being "good" isn't half as important as being there, eager to learn and enjoy.

Your relationship with your body will change. Perhaps your posture will be the first transformation. Then your expectations. When you think of yourself as an athlete, it might begin to seem perfectly normal — imperative, even — to devote time each day to physical fitness. After all, that's what athletes do. You'll begin to make more conscious choices about nutrition, stretching, strengthening, resting. You'll begin to feel competent to join a yoga class or bowling league or neighborhood Ping-Pong game — even if you don't win, even if you weigh more than you should, even if you're too embarrassed to say "I am an athlete" out loud. Over time, you might even become someone who is "trained or skilled in exercises, sports, or games requiring physical strength, agility or stamina." (See "K is for Knowledge" and "S is for Strong.")

But this is not really a book about joining a gym or starting a walking program. This is a book about how to approach life with an athletic sense of purpose, power, and possibility. It's about bringing athletic discipline, humility, and integrity into your everyday life. It's about claiming — or, for starters, simply trying on — an athletic identity, the way one might start to think of oneself as a singer, artist, healer, or smart, good, or loving person. "Athlete" is a useful, empowering identity. I know that not only because of my own experience, but because of feedback I receive from thousands of audience members who have heard me share this message. Exactly how that athletic mentality changes individuals — our perspective, our behavior, and perhaps also our bodies — is up to each of us.

The essentials

En route to lacrosse, field hockey, and basketball games while attending Shady Grove Junior High in Blue Bell, Pennsylvania, my teammates and I would sing on the bus. In this way, we amused ourselves on long rides all over eastern Pennsylvania, psyched ourselves up for games, and simply enjoyed being together. One of our standards was a chant:

"S-U-C-C-E-S-S.
That's the way you spell success!"

As a young writer, I took that more literally than most. Okay, so *that's* how you spell it, I thought, taking mental notes on those two "c's" and two final "s's." Having chanted it for hours, I felt confident I'd never spell it wrong. But I also asked myself, even then, sitting on that yellow school bus, how *do* you "spell" success?

I now believe that, just as a writer needs twenty-six letters of the alphabet, we need twenty-six athletic essentials to excel in everyday life. "Essential" means "so important as to be indispensable." These A to Z essentials are time-tested athletic methods for achieving peak performance.

Here's my promise: athletic essentials can help any person achieve success in any field: sports, media, politics, law, science, service, sales, entertainment, government, medicine, religion, teaching, trades, training, and more. Once you master them, you can spell success any way you wish.

Ten questions

Like athletes, all of us are playing a game with a clock. One day, our game will be over. The clock will stop. The lights will be turned off. Everyone will go home.

Exactly how much time do we have left in the game of our lives? We don't have control over that. We do have control over how we will play that game: how much joy and enthusiasm we will bring to the experience, what rules we will play by, and how we will treat our teammates, opponents, and fans.

Like athletes, all of us have bodies that need care and attention. We all have physical, intellectual, emotional, or spiritual dreams and goals. We all face situations in which we are tested. And we are all role models and leaders, whether we know it or not.

Here are ten questions to ask yourself about your game of life:

1) What is the point of this game? (Is it to accomplish things? To survive? To have fun? To create or procreate? To improve life for your loved ones or others? Or is it, as some pro athletes say, "just a job"?)

2) What's your goal?

3) What's your game plan?

4) Who are your teammates, and how will you relate to them?

5) Who are your opponents, and how will you relate to them?

> How much time do we have left in the game of our lives? We don't have control over that. We do have control over how we will play that game.

6) Who are your fans (the people who look to you for leadership), and how will you relate to them?

7) How will you strengthen, stretch, feed, and care for your body?

8) What rules will you play by?

9) How will you keep score?

10) How will you celebrate success?

How to use this book

Throughout this book, you will be asked to think of yourself as an athlete, and to decide for yourself how to spend these precious moments that are still left in your game of life. You will be asked to define for yourself what your goals are, who your teammates are, who your opponents are, how you want to relate to your body, what rules you're choosing to play by, and how you will keep score and measure success.

At the end of each chapter, you'll find a "Time Out for Reflection" section, where you'll be asked questions that will help you create a game plan for success. All of the questions, stories, and quotes in the book are designed to help you maximize your performance — and maximize your enjoyment of the game of life.

This book can be read by individuals, of course. It can also be used in a structured setting, as part of a leadership development program for professionals, athletes, students, or others who want to enhance their leadership skills. Each of the 26 chapters focuses on one quality essential not only to athletic success, but to success as a responsible mentor, teacher, manager, executive, or student leader. Learning to think like and act like an athlete is one way to think like and act like a leader.

Few of us think of ourselves as athletes. Even those who claim that identity often fail to bring those essentials into classrooms, emergency rooms, board rooms, boiler rooms, or rooms full of dinner guests.

If you already think of yourself as an athlete, this book will remind you what you have learned on the playing fields, and will show you how to apply these skills and concepts to anything you do.

If you do not think of yourself as an athlete, it's not too late to start. But if "athlete" still seems too wildly divergent from your self-perception, that's okay, too. Read on. Even if you were picked last for teams, even if you feel uncoordinated or out of shape, even if you're not particularly interested in your own physical potential, try integrating these 26 athletic essentials into your life on a daily basis. Before long, you'll be experiencing life as an athlete, behaving as an athlete — and having that much fun.

*   *   *   *   *

A is for Athlete

Think of yourself as an athlete. I guarantee you it will change the way you walk, the way you work, and the decisions you make about leadership, teamwork, and success.

A is for Athlete
Strong, brave, and fair
You could be all that
And more. If you dare.

"Do you think of yourself as an athlete?"

Everywhere I go, I ask people that question. Usually it comes up after someone mentions skating or swimming laps or playing golf or walking in malls.

"Well, I work out," they respond. Or,

"I'm into fitness," or,

"I try to stay in shape," or,

"I used to be a tomboy," or,

"I'm athletic, but not an athlete," or,

"No, I'm too lazy," or,

"No, because I'm not very fast or good or successful."

Even today, when more adults and children play sports than ever before, few of us say without apology or qualification: "Yes, I am an athlete."

A 42-year-old author I know skates forwards and backwards beautifully, has enjoyed skating for thirty years, and is teaching her young daughter to skate, but tells me she can't claim the word athlete "because I'm overweight and I just don't look like my idea of how an athlete should look."

How should an athlete look? Who should get to decide? How would your life change if you walked through the world with athletic pride, confidence, courage?

I encourage people to think of themselves as athletes not only because it changes their self-image, but because it changes their behavior. In my case, claiming the word athlete — and consciously applying my athletic wisdom to the rest of my life — enabled me to fulfill my childhood dream of becoming an author.

A childhood dream

I've always loved words, stories, and books. My mother used to read to us at night: Dr. Seuss's *Cat in the Hat*; A. A. Milne's *Winnie the Pooh*, with Christopher Robin, Eeyore, Kanga, Baby Roo, and the time Piglet was terrified of the Heffalump except the Heffalump turned out to be Pooh with his head stuck in a jar of honey; and Robert Louis Stephenson's *A Child's Garden of Verses*, with its iambic meter in this ode to the joy of that childhood sport known as swinging:

> *"How do you like to go up in a swing*
> *Up in the air so blue?*
> *Oh, I do think it the pleasantest thing*
> *Ever a child can do!"*

Books expressed the simple ecstasy of being alive — and also, sometimes, the silliness, like this from Ogden Nash:

> *"Shake, shake the ketchup bottle.*
> *None'll come, but then a lot'll."*

Some books offered useful and even profound advice, like this excerpt from a poem by Beatrice Schenk de Regniers:

*"Keep a poem in your pocket
and a picture in your head
and you'll never feel lonely
at night when you're in bed.*

*The little poem will sing to you
the little picture bring to you
a dozen dreams to dance to you
at night when you're in bed."*

One of my dreams, as I lay in bed, was to write a book. Since I was the third child in a family of three kids in a house with three bedrooms, there were no bedrooms left by the time I came along, so my parents put me in the room that had been my father's study before I was born. It was small, and when they moved me into it, they didn't take out my father's desk, his file cabinet, or the huge bookcases lined with books. Basically, I grew up in an office.

I would lie in bed listening to my mother's voice, gazing at the bookcase filled with books, and thinking, "I want to be an author." It seemed like the most marvelous thing in the world.

My brother Peter, two years older, came home from school each day and excitedly taught me what he had learned about grammar, punctuation, and spelling. By the time I was four, I was writing stories. One day I proudly showed Peter a story I had written. It was a sports story, about a family of beach balls. Peter said, "You can't be an author. You did it wrong."

"What do you mean?" I asked.

"You started in the *middle* of the story, with 'Mother Ball said, Let's do tricks,' he complained. "You have to start at the *beginning*, with 'Once upon a time.'"

I have since learned not to take anything the critics say too seriously — especially if they're only six years old. But at the time I was intimidated. In school, teachers further discouraged me. One said, "Okay, you want to be an author, but what are you going to do for a living?" She even cited statistics: "Fewer than five percent of all writers make a living at it."

I wanted to be in that five percent, but didn't know how. I didn't believe I could. I also couldn't envision what I would write about. No one was writing about the female experience of sports. Newspapers, magazines, and television shows almost never mentioned female athletes. And there weren't that many. Fewer than 300,000 girls played high school sports when I was growing up, compared to almost 3 million today. The year I started playing basketball at Stanford (1974), only one American woman, Annie Meyers, received an athletic scholarship. There was no Olympic women's basketball until 1976, and no professional women's basketball until 1978. So I had no role models, no way to imagine that my first book would be about how women are changing sports and sports are changing women.

> Wasn't there anything I had learned on the basketball court — or swimming pool, lacrosse field, ski slope — that I could apply to a career as a writer?

I kept reading and writing, but hid my journals in the bottom of my T-shirt drawer. At Stanford, I studied psychology and women's studies but avoided all the writing courses, afraid that someone else would tell me, as my brother had so many years before, that I was doing it wrong.

After college, I played pro basketball, then earned a masters in public health and served as a volunteer coordinator at a hospice. Caring for dying people is fascinating and meaningful work, but when I turned twenty-four, a line from Neil Young's "Old Man" started haunting me: "Twenty-four and there's so much more..." I found myself thinking: my life is passing quickly! Before I know it, I'm going to be 84 years old, looking back, and thinking, *I always wanted to be an author*.

I had spent countless hours perfecting my hook shot, my head fake, my baseline jumper. I knew how to snatch a sphere out of the sky as if I were saving a burning planet. I knew how to reverse pivot, fire a quick pass to the outlet, then flash into the lane on the fast break. But had I wasted my time? These skills had seemed vitally important then, but now seemed worthless.

Sure, I had enjoyed myself, made friends, won awards, and even supported myself as an athlete. Athletic involvement had given me an identity, a role in my family, a social support system, a profound confidence in my ability to achieve, and an appreciation for a very long, very lean body that might otherwise have seemed geeky. I knew that sports were more than just "fun and games."

But this was the early eighties, long before anyone would be impressed to see "played pro basketball" on a woman's resume. How, if at all, might the fact that I had been very good at shooting a large orange ball through a round iron rim help me *now*? With the pro league already defunct and my knees too sore to play anyway, did I really have to start over entirely to begin a new occupation? Wasn't there anything I had learned on the basketball court — or swimming pool, lacrosse field, ski slope — that I could apply to a career as a writer?

Suddenly I thought of this: I could practice. From the time I was in kindergarten I'd been practicing sports, so I knew in a visceral way not only how enjoyable practice can be, but how effective. This is such an elementary fact — *If you want to improve, practice* — but it had never occurred to me until then to practice writing the way I'd practiced sports.

I started writing every day. Because of sports, I had the self-discipline to create a schedule and stick to it, showing up at my desk even when I felt like bodysurfing instead.

Soon I heard my unique "voice" and began to develop it. Next I enrolled in writing classes, where I found a teacher, someone who would lead me through the next phase of my incipient writing career. As I had with sports coaches, I asked this woman — the poet and author Ellen Bass — to help me learn everything I possibly could. She did not disappoint.

In Ellen's classes I discovered other writing students. Teammates! These ambitious colleagues shared my passion for good writing and supported me as I pursued my goals.

When "Coach Bass" encouraged me to submit articles for publication, I felt honored and excited but also insecure. I'd never published anything. I hadn't attended journalism school — or even college writing classes. How could I compete with "real" writers whose bylines appeared in newspapers and magazines?

Again, my athletic frame of reference helped. Of course I could compete. I'd been competing my whole life. Still, the prospect of "losing" — having my work rejected — made my stomach clench like a fist. Yet this was the same way I had felt about an hour before basketball games. So it wasn't "fear" after all, as I had initially thought. I was simply "getting psyched up"!

Insecurity, I remembered, is a fleeting feeling, as ephemeral as the smoke from a starter's gun. It's simply what happens when athletes face new challenges. Next, they tap into something deeper and more substantial — their belief in their ability to succeed.

In this way, I began to apply some of the essentials I had learned from sports — goals, discipline, leadership, teamwork, and competitive spirit — to my writing.

When I did receive rejection notices (perhaps I should not have sent my first submissions to *The New Yorker*), I felt disappointed. But again I drew on my athletic experience, remembering that athletes don't stop playing when things don't go as planned. They notice what went wrong, rebound their own missed shots, seek new opportunities as well as new skills, and shoot again.

Athletes also set reasonable goals. When my first article was published, it was in a small, free, local women's newsmagazine (*Matrix*) in Santa Cruz, California.

Rebounding and writing

Now, many years later, I have achieved my childhood dream of becoming an author, having written five books, including this one. I've written hundreds of articles for publications like the *New York Times*, the *Washington Post*, *USA Today*, and *Newsweek*. I still practice writing almost every day. I still have coaches (writing mentors) and teammates (friends and colleagues who want me to succeed.) I still compete with other writers; that's simply the way of the world. And I still set new goals, which makes the process more focused and fun.

I still feel disappointed and defeated sometimes. But now that I'm in the habit of implementing athletic essentials, I remind myself that losing is part of the game of life. I tell myself to rebound. And I keep writing.

Regardless of how physically active you are, and regardless of what your sports experiences have been, try saying to yourself and to others, "I am an athlete." Identify with Wayne Gretzky, Sheryl Swoopes, Marion Jones, Kobe Bryant, Sergio Garcia, Jennifer Capriati, Apolo Anton Ohno, Michelle Kwan. See how intent they are on their goals, how willing they are to compete. See how quickly they recover when they blow it. Allow yourself to believe that you, too, could be that focused, that persistent, that cooperative, that competitive, that good at recovering from mistakes, on your job or in your school or at home.

Athletes learn how to deal with the pressure of limited time. Athletes practice and persist with specific objectives in mind. They receive instruction from a coach or teacher or mentor, and in turn they lead others. They're courageous, they're committed, and they're so confident and graceful that I can generally tell whether a person is athletic simply by observing their stride. Athletes walk with pride and joy, heads held high. They try new things. They understand that losing is simply something that happens on the way to success. No wonder employers often report that they prefer to hire people with athletic experience. Sports teach people how to make the most of life.

> No wonder employers often report that they prefer to hire people with athletic experience.

Henley Gabeau, a runner and former executive director of the Road Runners Club of America, reports, "Seeing myself as an athlete gives me the confidence to make changes and move on to new things. Running brings to the surface a sense of adventure, courage, leadership, and optimism. I'm always eager to see around the next curve or corner. This is true in life *and* on the running trail."

Recently I gave a speech to the National Association of Secondary School Principals. "Think of yourselves as athletes," I told them, then explained how and why to do so. Later that day, my friend and colleague Laurie Aomari happened to be in the hotel swimming pool when one of these high school principals walked onto the pool deck, dove into the water, surfaced, and introduced herself to Laurie by saying, "Hi. I'm Mary Smith, and I am an athlete!"

Sure enough, the administrator had heard me speak that morning, and had been so inspired she just had to skip one of the afternoon sessions to take a swim. Of course this was gratifying to hear.

What would happen if you thought of yourself as an athlete? What if, when faced with a challenging choice, you asked yourself, How would an athlete approach this situation?

A is for Athlete: Think of yourself as an athlete. I guarantee you it will change the way you walk, the way you work, and the decisions you make about leadership, teamwork, and success.

* * * * *

Time Out for Reflection

1) What is your primary identity, and how does that affect your behavior?

_____

_____

2) If you are not an athlete, when did you decide that?

_____

_____

3) If you are an athlete, how could you bring more of that mentality into your everyday life?

_____

_____

B is for B Game

Prepare to win on an off-day

B is for B Game
The one below A.
You can't always ace life
B Game's for off-days.

At the age of 21, Tiger Woods made a comment that was heard — and misunderstood — 'round the world. It was May 1997, and he had just won the GTE Byron Nelson Classic in Irving, Texas, his second victory in a row and his fifth win in his previous twelve appearances. The month before, Woods had won the Masters by a record 12 strokes, and his stunned colleagues on the tour were reeling.

Though he shot rounds of 64, 64, 67, and 68 for a record 17-under total at the Byron Nelson Classic, Woods explained that he won the event with "my C Game, surely not my A or B Game." Some of his fellow tour professionals, already daunted by Tiger's talent, believed he was belittling them. The way they heard it, Tiger might as well have taunted, "I could beat you guys with one hand tied behind my back."

"Tiger kept saying he didn't have his A Game this week," complained Lee Rinker, who finished two shots behind Woods. "What is his A Game, 40 under par?"

Tour veteran Brad Faxon took Tiger aside to caution him that his comments were not appreciated. "I told him he better be aware of what [he's] saying and how it affects your fellow guys," Faxon told *Golf Digest*. "I think he listened to me. He's the most impressive thing that's come along in a long time. He's got superb confidence, which is what any great player has. But if he wants people to like him, he's got to watch it."

Earl Woods, Tiger's father, jumped into the fray: "At the Masters, Tiger gave people a glimpse of his A Game for about two rounds. He showed that his A Game is too good for anybody else's A Game and proved that his B Game is better than most professionals' A Game."

Needless to say, this did nothing to mitigate the resentment.

Taking Faxon's advice, apparently, Woods now refrains from grading his games, though reporters continue to ask. A typical exchange more than five years later:

Reporter: "Would you say you played your A or B
Game today?"

Woods: "I'm playing pretty well."

You can't always hit the ball well

Here's what Tiger's peers failed to understand: Tiger was simply being honest — and insightful. "You can't go out there every day and hit the ball well. Every major championship, you always have one day where you're not going to hit the ball well," he explained after shooting a 70 at the PGA championship in 2000.

Tiger knows what he is capable of — hitting the ball well, to put it mildly — and he also knows that he cannot perform at that peak every day. No one can perform at their peak every day. So Woods has created a system for identifying the subtle changes in his game from day to day. Before being silenced by his rivals' accusations of arrogance, he mentioned 3 games: A, B, and C. Who knows how many more he may have in his repertoire? Perhaps all the way to Z.

What matters is that Woods has found a way to accept the inevitable vicissitudes of golf. He demonstrates a mature, even spiritual acceptance that one simply cannot play an A Game every day. This acceptance eludes some of Tiger's peers who sabotage their success with crippling self-recrimination or emotional outbursts when their A Game fails to materialize.

Other people do this too: frustrate themselves and undermine their own progress with unrealistic expectations. Successful people become successful in part because of high expectations, but those high expectations can get in the way when real (human, fallible, unpredictable) life intervenes.

> **Serenity is knowing that your worst shot is still going to be pretty good.**
>
> — legendary golfer Johnny Miller

Tiger's comments continue to reverberate around the globe, echoed by athletes, politicians, and businesspeople. Most focus on the A Game. University of Tennessee women's basketball coach Pat Head Summitt, anticipating her semi-final contest with eventual national champion University of Connecticut in the 2002 Final Four, said, "We've got to bring our A Game."

Republican Congressional Representative Robert L. Ehrlich, Jr., campaigning for governor of Maryland, pronounced, "As Tiger would say, I need to bring my A Game."

Sure, bring that A Game if you can. Visualize it, prepare for it, pack it up and tote it along if at all possible. But regardless of your work ethic and good intent, your A Game is not something you can necessarily bring, like a wallet. You can't control it like that. If you could, all performances would be peak performances, and that's not the case. We need only remember a series of polished figure skaters teetering and toppling onto the ice each Olympics to know that the A Game often does not obey.

Tiger's larger lesson involves the B (or even C) Game. His point: A person can be victorious even when things don't go as planned. (And how often do they?)

Three lessons from Tiger Woods

Here's what I think Tiger could teach us, if only we would listen:

1) Develop an A Game: the best that you can possibly be. Strive for this level of performance every day.

2) Accept that you cannot perform at the level of your A Game every day.

3) Develop a B Game — a utilitarian approach that is less beautiful, less stunning, less flashy, but dependable and effective. When you find that your A Game is not available, accept and even embrace this B or C Game, this backup plan. Trust, nurture, and appreciate this approach for what it is, and it too will lead to impressive and victorious results, at least some of the time. Legendary golfer Johnny Miller put it his way: "Serenity is knowing that your worst shot is still going to be pretty good."

Some people can't accept that their A Game will fail them. When it does, they fall apart. Others have no A Game. They aren't disciplined or dedicated enough to strive for excellence, and this becomes an excuse for mediocrity: "I'm not very good at this." It justifies laziness: "Since I'm not very good, I have no "best shot" to give."

And many of us have no B Game, no way to stay focused and confident when things are not going well. Yet that's life. It refuses to proceed in the exact way we envision it. Some days we have a cold. Some days we feel tired. Despite our efforts to stay in top mental and physical condition, we can't always produce an A Game. That's why the B game is so important, and so useful.

Bringing the B Game to the stage

Recently I gave a speech in Hawaii. It was the first of three speeches on my schedule there, and I had looked forward to my "paid vacation" at a luxury resort on Oahu. But something happened at that first speech that has not happened to me in more than fifteen years of professional speaking: The audience refused to enter the room. The room was too cold, they said. They staged an impromptu boycott, loitering in the hall while I scrambled to find the meeting planner.

One thing professional speakers do is control the ambiance as much as possible. So I had visited the room earlier that morning to test the microphones and the VCR, and to check the podium, lectern, lighting, and chairs. Because the chairs had been mistakenly set in straight rows, rather than curved rows, as I had requested (curved rows make audiences more comfortable, and thus tend to make the event more enjoyable for everyone), I had personally rearranged about 300 chairs. Perhaps working up a sweat during that process, I had failed to notice the chilly room temperature.

Other things had also gone wrong. On the way to Hawaii from Washington, D.C., I got locked out of Los Angeles International Airport with thousands of other travelers because of a security breach. We stood outside for almost four hours, waiting. Then, while I was chewing on a granola bar, a crown in my mouth came loose. I lost it. The airline lost (then found) my luggage. After I finally arrived in Hawaii, attended a reception, unpacked, and went to sleep, I was awakened in the middle of the night because it was raining — in my room. A window was leaking badly, and drops of water were loudly splashing into a puddle on my rug. Unable to sleep through the noise, I called the front desk and changed rooms in the middle of the night, which involved packing and unpacking all over again. In the morning I developed an inner ear infection. Not only did I suffer from a deep, painful headache, I felt dizzy. Every time I moved my head, it seemed I'd just spun around in a triple lutz.

All frequent fliers deal with travel hassles. We learn to live with them and laugh about them. But this was a bit much. Even two days later, preparing to deliver the first speech, I felt tired, headachy, and dizzy. So when the audience boycotted, I noticed that, for the first time in my life, I actually felt angry with them. Not a good sign. I knew the anger was misplaced (the audience was not responsible for any of my woes), but just noticing it in myself was unsettling.

I finally found someone who turned off the air conditioning. The audience members entered the room and sat down.

But, not surprisingly, I was unable to deliver my A Game speech. I simply could not summon the physical or emotional resources to be quite as engaging, amusing, and involved with the audience as I usually am. Between the ear infection and the fatigue, my timing was off.

> **Accept that you cannot perform at the level of your A Game every day.**

Fortunately for me, this was a new audience, so they couldn't compare my performance to past performances. And fortunately for all of us, I have come to accept that I can't always be perfectly "on," and have learned to proceed anyway, as if I'm "on," so that others don't notice. I believe — and evaluations confirmed — that my B Game speech was well received. They even gave me a standing ovation.

Actors develop this skill. They take the stage and perform brilliantly despite colds, flu, heartache, fear, grieving, and boredom. Night after night, they make their characters come alive, even when they themselves would rather be home in bed. The best actors deliver consistently, without ever letting us know whether we're seeing their A Game or B Game.

We owe it to our clients, our colleagues, our protegees, and our families to stay focused and determined, even when only our B game shows up. Our discipline and training should help us stay so calm in the face of distractions, discomfort, and unpredictable performance that only we will notice which game we are playing. A lot to strive for? Yes. Worth striving for? Yes.

I also think of this as the "Be Game." It's about accepting the way things are, and giving it your best shot, regardless.

B is for B Game: Prepare to win on an off day.

*   *   *   *   *

TIME OUT FOR REFLECTION

1) Name one aspect of your life in which you have an A Game.

   _____

   _____

2) Can you think of a time in which your A Game failed you, yet you still succeeded? What happened?

   _____

   _____

3) What could you do to develop and gain more confidence in your B Game?

   _____

   _____

C is for
Competitive Spirit

Welcome challenges and rise to the occasion

C is for Competitive
The will and the way
To test yourself, take risks.
Life's a game. Play.

W hen the University of Connecticut women's basketball team traveled to rival University of Tennessee's home court in early 2002 for their first game that year, the Knoxville gym was filled with an NCAA record-setting 24,611 fans, most of them dressed in Tennessee orange. Diana Taurasi, a Connecticut guard who scored a career-high 32 points to propel her team to an 86-72 victory, explained her pre-game attitude this way: "Yeah, I was a little more pumped for today. You see 25,000 people out there rooting against you — it's a great feeling."

This is something athletes understand. It's a great feeling to try to accomplish something when others want you to fail. This is what rising to meet challenges is about: using opposition as a motivating and energizing force. And this is what competition is about: striving to meet an objective while other people strive to prevent you from meeting that objective. It can be scary, difficult, unpleasant, disappointing, even humiliating. It can also be tremendous fun. The key is to understand that, whether the competition takes place on or off the playing fields, it's just a game.

The Mom story

It was my mother who taught me to welcome challenges and rise to the occasion. The first time Mom and I competed against each other, I was 5 years old. She was 37. We swam one lap of our neighbor's pool. She won.

> The most significant common intangible among the truly great is that they enjoy adversity.
>
> — golfer Gary Player

Mom has always been a good swimmer, but like many women of her generation she didn't have anyone to compare herself to. She swam laps — but that gets boring. So she'd secretly race against the person in the next lane.

Once, when I was sitting on a bench at the YWCA waiting for Mom, I watched her furiously churning the water in Lane One while some unsuspecting person in Lane Two was innocently swimming laps. When they reached the end, Mom slapped her hand on the tile and said, "Ha! Beat you!" She was not very popular at the Y.

I kid Mom that that's why she had children. Having failed to find suitable rivals, Mom decided to create some. But Mom's first child, my sister Carol, had no interest in sports, so Mom had to keep having kids. Next she had my brother. Peter loved baseball, but he had ear problems, so he couldn't swim. Next, I was born, so finally, Mom could stop having kids, because I loved almost every sport, including swimming, and was perfectly happy to race against Mom.

I remember what I wore to our first race: a new tan bathing suit with a pink skirt that poked out like a ballerina's tutu. I swear my mother bought this for me because she knew it would increase drag in the water, thus slowing me down.

My father, standing on the edge of the pool, said, "Ready, set, GO!"

(This is an interesting series of questions and commands: 1) Are you ready? Have you done everything you possibly can to prepare for this moment? 2) Are you set? Are you balanced, centered, focused? 3) Now, go! Don't doubt yourself or your plans or approach. Just go!)

I went, diving in and swimming as fast as I could. When I reached the end, I looked over at Mom. I could tell she had already been there for a while. Just to make sure I knew, she slapped the end of the pool and said, "Ha! Beat you!"

When I tell this story in public, earnest parents often ask me afterward, "Do you recommend competing against young children like that?"

It depends — on the child, on his or her age and ability level, and on the relationship. Of course you wouldn't want to demoralize a child by repeatedly beating them handily.

But no one had told me that losing was a bad thing. No one told me that "Ha! Beat you!" was cruel. It didn't feel cruel. It felt playful. There was Mom, her eyes red from chlorine, her face beaming. How could I be anything but happy? I was swimming, I was playing a game with Mom, and I was learning to enjoy adversity.

"The most significant common intangible among the truly great," says golfer Gary Player, "is that they enjoy adversity."

On the other hand, I was not a fool. I could see that Mom was having *more* fun than I was. I intuitively understood this fact: winning is more fun than losing.

So I chose my first goal: To beat Mom in what became an annual tradition: one length of our neighbor's pool — no handicaps, no head starts, no cheating. Ready, set, GO!

To train for this event, I joined a swim team. On that team I found a coach: someone who expected us to show up for practice every day, even if we'd rather be at a birthday party. On that team I found teammates: Jean and Joan, the famous Spinelli twins of Blue Bell, Pennsylvania. They were my age and a lot faster but very nice about it. I would chase them in practice, trying to stay near their feet.

On that team I learned to do a racing dive: to soar out over the water, then slip through one single hole in the surface, sleek and graceful as a dolphin. I learned to roll from side to side the way marine mammals do, extending each arm to minimize stroke count and maximize hydrodynamic efficiency. I ditched the ballerina tutu and squeezed into my first team Speedo, green with black and white racing stripes. And I learned to walk onto the pool deck with pride, head held high, chest out — not to psyche out the opponent, but because that's what you do, that's how you walk, that's how proud and confident you feel, when you're an athlete.

While Mom was busy working (she's a physician), I kept training. I acquired race experience, competing with the six-and-unders, then the eight-and-unders, then the ten-and-unders.

The year I was six, Mom won again. She won when I was seven, eight, and nine. But each year I grew a little older, taller, faster, and stronger, and each year I got a little closer to beating Mom. I continued to crave what she had: success.

The year I was ten, I finally beat Mom. She disputes this now, maintaining that I was eleven. But I remember that race too — including what I said afterward: "Ha! Beat you!"

When I think about competition I remember the Spinelli twins, who would join me in the showers after the meets, the three of us giggling and whispering until all the hot water ran out. When I think about competition I remember my six-foot-three-inch basketball teammate, Heidi Wayment, who played with me on a pro team in France and rebounded the ball viciously, sharp elbows out. I hated her elbows but loved her audacity and her long strong hands, mirrors of my own.

When I think about competition I realize that by introducing me to sports and by never letting me win, my mother — who at 55 took up tennis, at 60 tried downhill skiing, and at 70 became a scuba diver— showed me what it means to have a competitive spirit, and demonstrated how much fun that can be.

Lisa Ryerson, president of Wells College in Aurora, New York, says her competitive experiences helped her become the nation's youngest college president (at 35). She comes from a family of six children: five girls, then a boy. "We were highly competitive in every arena: academics, athletics, and music too," recalls Ryerson, the fourth child. In junior high and high school, Lisa and a younger sister competed on the debate team. "It became very important for us. We did a lot of research and work. There were boys who didn't want to compete against us, who would say negative things about 'those competitive Marsh sisters.' I can't remember how we responded to them. Except that we went ahead and won. Stood up and grabbed the trophy."

Competing versus having fun

"Should children play competitive sports? Or should they just play to have fun?" That's a question I often hear from parents.

My answer: Yes. Children should be exposed to competitive sports — which can be lots of fun. Of course children should also be exposed to noncompetitive physical activities such as T'ai Chi, aikido, yoga, hiking, horseback riding, and all sorts of dance. They should have free time to build forts and climb trees and lie on the grass, watching clouds drift by. But parents are mistaken when they think that the fun will drain out of activities as soon as someone starts keeping score.

> Competing can be scary, but that doesn't mean you shouldn't do it.

In fact, the fun begins with mastery. Teach kids to throw, kick, climb, swim, and run, and they'll enjoy a sense of accomplishment. Only then, after they've developed some skills, should they begin competing. At that point, they'll need adult guidance to help them figure out how and why to keep score. What does winning mean? What does losing mean? In what ways do they matter, and in what ways do they not matter? Does winning entitle you to gloat? Is it worth cheating for? Or is it just a helpful goal?

Of course these are important questions for adults to answer for themselves, too, regardless of whether they have children. (See "W is for Winning.")

Competition gets easier over time

Over time, this process — taking risks, making mistakes, taking more risks, grabbing the trophy — gets easier, because you remember something Mom showed me: the challenge itself is fun. It's fun to get ready, get set, then go, not knowing who will win a race. It's fun to fly out over the water then swerve through it, pretending to be a marine mammal. Twenty-five thousand people are rooting against you? So much the better. This is the competitive spirit that leads to success in sports, in business, in a televised debate, in a piano competition, and beyond.

To compete is to risk failing, looking foolish, feeling disappointed, not living up to your own expectations, not living up to society's expectations of how and where and with whom you "should" compete. To compete is to risk winning and feeling guilty or embarrassed or undeserving or pressured to win again. To compete is to risk learning what you can achieve and what you can't.

It can be scary, but that doesn't mean you shouldn't do it. "I've been terrified every moment of my life, and I've never let it keep me from doing a single thing I've wanted to do," said the great painter Georgia O'Keefe.

Athletes say "yes" to tests, games, competitions, and other opportunities to excel. They welcome challenges for their own sake, for their inherent excitement and unpredictable outcome, accepting that they will sometimes fail and sometimes succeed. They allow themselves to exert extreme effort — without losing perspective that life is just a game. They welcome the audience, the clock, the opponent, and the deadline: external pressures that add intensity and meaning. They use the pressure of public accountability to strive for peak performance.

Athletes also learn to compete in a more low-keyed way, striving to break barriers but not holding it against themselves, or even necessarily remembering, when they don't. A runner tries to better his time in practice, but feels no significant disappointment if the time is not lowered. Setting a competitive challenge simply makes the practice more interesting. A teacher strives to be the best teacher in the school, but doesn't pout if a peer wins Best Teacher accolades instead. Since we can't always win, an important part of competition is taking failure in stride, and keeping the entire game in perspective.

To compete is to commit yourself, to say: I want to win, and I'm willing to try. To compete is to thrive on challenge. To feel the pressure, and embrace it.

Update on Mom

Mom and I still compete when I visit her in Phoenix. She has her own backyard pool, and we race there. I give her a head start. She never gave me a head start, but I claim to be nicer than she is. Besides, fair is fair. I'm a lot faster, and competitions are much more fun when they're close. So I swim three laps to her two, or whatever. She still gloats when she wins. "Ha! Beat you!" But believe me, I never let her win.

For many years now, I've been telling Mom about masters swimming. It's a marvelous program that gives people opportunities to compete against other people of their same age and gender. I started training and competing in masters swimming in the mid-eighties, after my knees disintegrated, and I love it. "Look, Mom, you'd love it too!" I said for years. I'd explain: "You only compete against people your own age, in five-year increments, such as 50-54, 55-59, 60-64. It would be fun. You'd love it!"

Mom always said, "But I'm not very fast. I wouldn't win."

And I'd say: "*Mom*! It's not about winning. It's about competing, playfully, to discover what you're capable of achieving. It's about enjoying your teammates, your opponents, and your own strength and grace. It would be fun, trust me!"

But she was afraid, as so many of us are afraid to dive into unfamiliar waters. Finally, one time when Mom came to visit me in Virginia, I woke her up early and drove her to my practice, where I work out with women and men of all ages. We train according to speed, with fast college kids in Lane One, mostly-middle-aged athletes in the middle lanes, and slow septuagenarians in Lane Six. I'm in Lane Three. I sent Mom over to Lane Six, where she met Helen and Lorraine, who are both about her age. Mom was able to keep up with them. They said, "Gee, Sarah, you're really fast!" That boosted her confidence.

She began to think, "Maybe I could win after all." When she returned to Phoenix, she joined the Phoenix Masters and began training with them. But she didn't enter her first meet that first year, when she was 69. She waited until she turned 70, so she'd be in the bottom of her age group, not having to compete against all those speedy 65- to 69-year-olds.

Before her first meet, she was so nervous she asked me if she should take "just one quarter of one Valium." I said no. She managed her nerves until she stepped onto the starting blocks, at which point her husband, Bernie, ran up to her.

"What's the matter?" she said impatiently. The starter, holding his pistol aloft, stared at the scene.

"Sarah," said Bernie, "you forgot to remove your shoes!"

Mom won that first race. She has gone on to win more gold medals than she can keep track of, in the Arizona State Championships, the Senior Olympics, and other events. She has placed as high as fourth in the nation, and currently holds two Arizona State breaststroke records for women aged 75-79.

Long gone are her "old lady" suits, plastic-flower caps, and the half-mile (800 meters) she used to paddle for fitness. She logs up to 2400 meters per workout, at timed intervals. She swims in a slick Speedo, packs her bag with goggles, fins, pull buoy, and chamois towel. She's even weight training now. If you meet her at a party, she'll insist you squeeze her biceps. "Sarah, you're a warrior!" her personal trainer said recently.

"I'm tickled pink!" she told me on the phone that day. Perhaps the world's first pink warrior.

Here's the moral of this story: If you know someone who wants to compete but is afraid, take her by the hand. Show her how exciting a new competitive environment can be. Introduce her around. Listen to her excuses and protests, but don't take any of that too seriously. Even potential champions sometimes need someone else to lead the way.

C is for Competitive Spirit: Welcome challenges and rise to the occasion.

* * * * *

TIME OUT FOR REFLECTION

1) What did you learn at an early age about competition?

_____

_____

2) When have you risen to a challenge?

_____

_____

3) Describe a specific situation in which you're competing with someone right now. (Hint: Who seems to be competing with you?)

_____

_____

D is for Discipline

Develop the habit of greatness

D is for Discipline
Practice rehearsing
Whether you're teaching or
Painting or nursing.

When I was twelve, my parents installed a basketball hoop in our driveway for my brother. Pete preferred baseball. I was the one who fell in love with basketball: the ball itself, the round, inviting hoop, the intricate but simple game, my teammates, my coaches, the entire improvisational dance. Even before I met my first team, when I was alone out there in the driveway, I was already in love. I'd caress the ball as it whirled under my palm, guiding it around the cars and potholes. I taught myself to shoot, aiming high so the brown leather sun would sink through the hole quietly, with no ambivalence. I adored the feel of the ball as it spun softly under my hands; the easy arch of the shot; the sweet satisfaction of the swish.

After hours of reverent, solitary play, I'd wash the ball in our basement sink, carefully rinsing away the driveway's gravel or snow. Later, lying in bed, I'd spin it straight overhead, trying to make it kiss the orange-spotted ceiling before settling in my happy hands. In the morning before school, I'd bounce my beloved off my bedroom wall, one hundred little taps with my right hand, one hundred with my left.

As I devoted myself to this basketball, learning to shoot it, catch it, pass it, and care for it, the basketball in return seemed to caress, care for, and even shape me, stretching my fingers, strengthening my willowy arms and legs, widening and lengthening my feet so they'd offer a good place from which I could jump, and on which I could land. Basketball became a gift I could share with friends and strangers. "Here! I'll pass you the ball!" As I grew ever upward, toward the basket, my body itself began to speak of the sport, so that my very presence in a room — head near the ceiling — would prompt people to ask, "Do you play basketball?"

> I'm a great believer in luck, and I find the harder I work, the more I have of it.
>
> — Thomas Jefferson

(Later, as my hair began to turn gray, the question became, "*Did* you play basketball?")

The summer before I entered Shady Grove Junior High as a seventh-grader, I found myself alone out there day after day, practicing my lay-ups, preparing to make the team. I worked out the footing step by step. Bounce the ball once with the right hand while stepping with the left foot; pick up the ball and take a step with your right; then another step with your left; leap off that foot toward the basket; shoot with the right hand. Arduously, I worked out the footing on the left side. Dribble left while stepping right, pick up the dribble, step left, step right, now jump off that right foot and shoot with the left hand. There! Wow! It went in!

Every day I shot a hundred lay-ups with my right hand, then a hundred with my left. I was serious about it, and systematic. I was working toward a goal but I also found the practice itself fascinating and rewarding.

When autumn came, I made the team and scored 14 points in my first game. The entire other team scored thirteen.

I was ecstatic. I was also surprised, because making the team had been easy. Scoring points was easy. Apparently I was better than the other junior high girls. How did that happen? After that first game, some of the kids on the other team sauntered over to congratulate me, and to ask me the same question that was on my mind.

"How did you get to be so good?" they asked.

I couldn't think of a reason, so I didn't say anything. They started musing aloud, "It's because she's tall. It must be because she's tall."

They had a point. At twelve, I was already five-seven. But finally I figured out the reason. "It's not because I'm tall," I corrected them. "It's because I've been *practicing*."

I didn't understand why the other girls hadn't spent that year practicing too.

Now I see. I was already an athlete. Having swum in meets since the age of six, I knew something the other girls didn't: how to discipline myself to achieve goals. It's really quite simple. You show up every day, even if you're tired or inclined to do something else. You dive into the water, even if it's chilly. You repeatedly rehearse, committing yourself to become the best you can possibly be. Excellence becomes a habit, as natural and necessary as tooth-brushing.

Whether playing softball, playing the piano, or playing around with a computer program, discipline yourself to get dressed, get ready, show up, and rehearse, over and over. Practice isn't always fun, but it often is. In any case, it's required. Good intentions yield results only when acted upon.

Mostly, it's a matter of hard work. "I'm a great believer in luck," Thomas Jefferson said, "and I find the harder I work, the more I have of it."

Said Charles Dickens, "I never could have done without the habits of punctuality, order and diligence...the determination to concentrate myself on one subject at a time."

The path to success is orderly

To children, "discipline" often has a negative connotation. It means getting punished. But wise parents use discipline as a way to help children control themselves, complete tasks, and display appropriate behavior. Clear rules about what's right and what's wrong, clear expectations, and clear guidelines about when and how homework should be accomplished, for instance, help children acquire the self-discipline they'll ultimately need to achieve their own goals.

Of all the lessons I've learned on the playing fields, discipline is the one I cherish the most, and for which I am most grateful to my many coaches. Though the path to success may be complicated or circuitous, it's orderly: one step at a time, over and over, until a goal is reached. It's amazing how many people don't understand this.

"People seldom see the halting and painful steps by which the most insignificant success is achieved," noted Annie Sullivan, Helen Keller's teacher and friend.

"I want to be a writer," people tell me.

"What sorts of things do you write?" I might ask.

"Well...." they say, "It's all in my head. I haven't actually written anything down yet." What they're describing is thinking, not writing. Unless they write — unless they discipline themselves to sit down and practice writing — they will never achieve their dream. It's as simple as this: People who practice improve.

From former athletes, I hear this lament: "I used to get up early every day and row, but now that I'm not in college..." Or, "I used to lift weights, and I felt great, but then I got out of the habit..."

Habit is everything. Keep in mind that inertia, while most commonly used to refer to the fact that "objects at rest stay at rest," also means that "objects in motion stay in motion." In other words, once you get going, you'll enjoy some forward momentum that will help you maintain the habit of excellence.

As an author, I'm in the habit of writing. As a speaker, I practice speaking. As a board member, I practice leadership. Every time I succeed at anything, it's because I've brought to that particular endeavor discipline: an orderly series of behaviors designed to achieve results.

The same is true for inner peace. There are many paths to peace, but all have one thing in common: discipline. Some people pray. Others meditate. Some spend time with nature. Some read poetry, or favorite sayings or teachings. Some listen to or create music. Many daily rituals can lead to results. But one prayer now and then probably won't do it. Nor will an occasional walk in the woods. The people who exhibit the most inner calm, it seems to me, are those who make their spiritual training a habit, a daily discipline. They practice the peace they want to achieve.

As Paul says in First Corinthians (9:24-27):

"Remember that in a race, everyone runs, but only one person gets the prize. You also must run in such a way that you will win. All athletes practice strict self-control. They do it to win a prize that will fade away, but we do it for an eternal prize. So I run straight to the goal with purpose in every step. I am not just shadowboxing. I discipline my body like an athlete, training it to do what it should. Otherwise, I fear that after preaching to others I myself might be disqualified."

There's an old adage: Practice makes perfect. Some coaches have changed it to "perfect practice makes perfect." I don't believe either one. Practice doesn't have to be perfect. It rarely is. If the skill had been perfected, it wouldn't need practice.

Practice should be playful. It's a creative experiment, during which you try out new ideas, behaviors, options. During this process of practicing you learn, change, become more proficient, figure out how to make it work for you. You practice because you're *not* perfect, and if it's an endeavor worth pursuing throughout one's life, it will never be perfected. It's the pursuit of excellence that's intriguing, chal-

> In order to enjoy a long, successful career, you must not only tolerate repetition, you must find beauty and meaning within continuous practice.
> — Chris Gekker, trumpet player

lenging, fun, and even thrilling, regardless of whether the original goal is ever attained.

Practice should also be deliberate. Over the years I met many basketball players who spent hours practicing half-court shots on the off chance that someday they would be called upon to win a game at the buzzer by launching one of these heavy satellites into orbit. They weren't practicing so much as playing — it can be fun to try outrageous shots in basketball — and I never begrudged them their fun. But if they fooled themselves into thinking it was a practical use of their time, they were wrong. I remember watching one high school teammate hurling half-court shots over and over, and wishing she would practice more free throws instead. I was not surprised when she dropped off the team.

Athletes usually practice in "progressions," wherein complex skills are simplified into a series of steps, as I did with the lay-ups in my driveway. Musicians do the same. A piano player begins with just a few fingers on a few keys, over and over, before progressing to more complicated material. The theory is that any skill can be mastered if it is first understood in its component parts.

Attention matters too. Practice can become so routine it's robotic, but high achievers resist the urge to sleep through their workouts. Golfer Ernie Els, describing a slump he suffered through in 2001, told the *Washington Post*, "I was doing a lot of practicing, but I was just doing mindless practicing. I thought the more balls I hit, the quicker I'll get out of it; things will just come right. I was wrong. I should have stood back, taken a few weeks off and come back fresh."

Every putt becomes a little lesson in itself

Recently I took a golf lesson from Julieta Stack, an LPGA teaching pro. I asked if she could help me read greens so I could predict how a ball will roll across an uneven surface. She said no.

"But you can teach yourself," she added. "Every time you putt, decide what path you expect the ball to take, then hit it, then watch what happens. In this way, every putt becomes a little lesson in itself."

Her advice reminded me of Chris Gekker, one of the world's best classical trumpet players. A professor at the University of Maryland, Gekker is a former member of the American Brass Quintet and the St. Luke's Chamber Orchestra. He has given solo performances in Carnegie Hall. Composers write music just for him. After more than thirty years of playing trumpet, he still practices every day — not only to stay in physical condition (the trumpet requires tremendous lung power as well as delicate lip and tongue control), but to learn more about himself and his music. To improve.

"In order to enjoy a long, successful career, you must not only tolerate repetition, you must find beauty and meaning within continuous practice," he says. "For the best players, at the times of their most intense practice, each scale, each phrase is like a little mirror. Every practice session becomes a little lesson they are giving themselves."

Not all of his students understand this. "If you go away for a week, please take your trumpet with you, even if you're on vacation," Gekker advises his students.

"Some of them are shocked," Gekker explains. "They ask, 'Isn't that unreasonable?' I agree that it is unreasonable. I tell them they don't have to. I say, 'You're a very good trumpet player, and you can be very good without disciplining yourself to practice every day. You just can't be a professional musician.'"

Discipline is what differentiates successful people from those who only dream about success. It's about putting one foot in front of the other, carefully and deliberately, learning from each step along the way. It's about sitting at the computer, writing, even when you don't believe you have anything brilliant or creative to say. Self-disciplined people get better at running, at writing, at whatever they practice. By rehearsing the same skills over and over, an activity that could be boring instead becomes meaningful, intense, challenging, and fun.

D is for Discipline: Develop the habit of greatness.

* * * * *

TIME OUT FOR REFLECTION

1) Describe a time when you practiced something and it paid off.

   _____

   _____

2) How would you rate your own self-discipline, on a scale of one to ten?

   _____

   _____

3) What would be two specific rewards you would receive if you were more self-disciplined?

   _____

   _____

4) How and when will you practice the skills needed to achieve your next goal?

   _____

   _____

E is for Endurance

Master the Power/Rest cycle

E is for Endurance
The trick is to rest
Then power, then rest
Again. That rhythm's best.

In 1999, I wrote an article for *Newsweek*. The US national soccer team had just won the Women's World Cup in a dramatic overtime victory witnessed by more than 90,000 fans in Pasadena, California, and millions more on television. Called "Learning What 'Team' Really Means," the essay explains why fans are excited about the success of women's team sports. I wrote the story on deadline, submitted it, then drove to Rehoboth, Delaware, for a previously scheduled week's vacation.

On its cover, *Newsweek* ran what became a famous photo of an exultant Brandi Chastain wearing only her sports bra and shorts, muscles rippling. That same day, a producer from the *Today* show called and asked me to appear the following morning with Brandi, Mia Hamm, and several of their teammates. The players would talk about their experiences winning the World Cup. My role would be to put their victory in a larger context: how women are changing sports and sports are changing women.

"Sorry, I'm on vacation," I said.

"Where?" asked the producer. She seemed to be imagining Greece, Acapulco, African safari.

"Uh, Delaware," I said.

"Can't you get from Delaware to New York tonight, so you can appear on the show tomorrow?" she asked, incredulous.

"Well, I could," I said, "but — I'm on vacation. This is my time for rest, reflection, renewal, reading, swimming, and golf."

"Maybe you don't understand," she said. "This is the *Today* show."

"I do understand, and I appreciate your invitation, and I hope you keep my name in your database and call back some time," I said. Then I proceeded to enjoy a wonderful week with my partner, our dog, and lots of sunshine, ocean swimming, and golf.

When I returned to work, I mentioned the incident to my mastermind group (colleagues who meet once a month to share ideas and support). They thought I was nuts. Who in their right mind turns down an invitation to appear on national television? Isn't this how authors sell books, speakers become celebrities, and ordinary people achieve their dreams of becoming famous?

Maybe I am nuts, but I'm happy. Fame for its own sake has never appealed to me. And while television appearances can boost one's business, I've appeared on television enough to know that it's not necessarily financially rewarding. I've also lived long enough to know that boosting one's business is not always the highest priority. There's a lot to be said for commitment to one's family.

I lead a balanced life. (Not perfectly balanced, but balanced.) I'm in a close longterm relationship. I spend time with friends. I read books. I play sports. I serve my community. I'm almost never sick, which might be related to the fact that I don't ride a constant roller coaster of stress. I love my work, but I don't work all the time. In fact, in addition to formal vacations, I spend time every day "on vacation": not answering the phone, not reading email, not planning or achieving or doing anything productive. Just walking outside in a cool breeze. Petting Rocky (my dog.) Dreaming.

I've been writing and speaking fulltime since 1987. That's a long time to be self-employed. People often tell me they couldn't discipline themselves to work when they don't feel like it. They would work too little, they say, or too much. They would burn out without the external structure of a "real job." It's not always easy for me either, and there are times when I do feel overwhelmed and exhausted. But fortunately, I know some things from sports about endurance: the ability to keep going over time, or to withstand hardship, adversity, or stress.

Henley Gabeau, marathoner and mother of two grown daughters, says the endurance she acquired through running helped her get perspective on parenting. "In training for a marathon, some of the runs you've plotted will be interrupted by illness or sore muscles," says Gabeau. "Yet you stay focused on the goal of successfully completing 26.2 miles.

"Parenting is the same. The discipline meted out, the examples set for a child of five, the helping with homework, the playing of games, the heartbreak of a teenager's skipped school days or lapse into drugs — all are focused on the child and your

> When rowers "rush the slide," lurching the seat forward in their eagerness to begin the next stroke, they not only upset the boat's balance, they actually jerk it in the wrong direction.

longterm vision of helping her become a caring, responsible, successful adult. Somehow you *know* you're going to complete that 26.2 miles without stopping, and somehow you *know* that that child will emerge as a fine young woman. You know it, and you stay focused on the longterm goal, and eventually she emerges as a young adult you're so proud of."

A man named Martin works as a manager at a large financial institution, and competes in triathlons in his spare time. "Sometimes during the marathon part of the triathlon, you're so tired you can't even think about the goal," he says. "You just put one foot in front of the other, enduring. My wife and I were stuck in the airport in a snowstorm one time, and had to sleep on the floor. I was cold, stiff and miserable, but I said to myself, 'You can do this. Just one step at a time, like triathlons.' I find that to be a very useful way to approach life."

Two keys to developing endurance

These are the two keys to developing endurance:

1) Patiently persisting, even when times are tough; and
2) Insisting on your right to rest, even when others tell you to keep going.

Athletes recognize this paradoxical pair as the Power/Rest cycle. This is the natural and essential rhythm of exertion and rest that is fundamental to any form of athletic — or other — success. The Power/Rest concept is simple: every energy expenditure must be followed by short-term or long-term rest. The skier powers down the mountain, then kicks back on the chair lift. She skis all day, then sleeps late the next morning. She skis for three days, then returns home.

The Power/Rest cycle is structured into most games. Basketball players, fatigued from running and jumping, can look forward to resting when the whistle blows for violations, fouls, time-outs, and halftime. Tennis players are permitted a few seconds between points, then a few minutes between games. Sprinters run for ten seconds, then stop and gasp for breath.

The Power/Rest cycle is also structured into athletes' daily, weekly, and monthly rhythms. Weightlifters are advised to lift only on alternate days, so the muscles can recover from the strain. Olympic athletes in virtually all sports rest at least one day a week. Marathoners almost never run marathons closer than a few weeks or even a few months apart.

Athletes learn to pace themselves, listening to their subtle internal rhythms so they can adjust Power/Rest schedules as needs arise. They stay conscious during the power phase, and during the rest phase, continually asking themselves, "Am I tired? So tired I need a break? Am I pushing hard enough? Too hard?"

The Power/Rest cycle is also integral to biomechanical movement. For your biceps to flex, your triceps must relax. When engaged in a motion (such as ball-throwing) that requires both the biceps and triceps to contract, the two muscles take turns.

In rowing, the "power" phase is called the "drive." Rowers dip their oars into the water, push with their legs, and pull with their arms. The "rest" period is called the "recovery." Rowers gently slide forward on their seats, oars out of the water, giving their lungs and muscles a much-needed respite — while preparing for the power phase again. This is not complete rest, like sleep. It's a rest that requires control, balance, attention, and focus — which makes it challenging.

> For ambitious people, it's tempting to work non-stop. We're not working hard, necessarily, but we're working all the time, and even when we're not working, we're worrying.

One common mistake rowers make is to "rush the slide." Willing to work hard to achieve their goals, they lose sight of the cyclical nature of Power/Rest, and try to Power/Power instead. When they do this, lurching the seat forward in their eagerness to begin the next stroke, they not only upset the boat's balance, they actually jerk it in the wrong direction.

So too with high achievers in any walk of life. Some of us fail because of too little power — lack of commitment, discipline, plain hard work. But others fail because of too little rest. In our efforts to keep powering through life, we jerk our own little boats in the wrong direction, allowing irritability or sloppiness to steer us off-course.

Holidays and vacations offer official "rest" time for people to stop working and celebrate love, family, faith, friendship, and everything we have to be grateful for. But increasingly, people interrupt holidays and vacations with cell phones, email, and other "urgent" responsibilities.

Some people must work virtually non-stop. Taxi drivers, maids, and waiters usually don't have the luxury of long vacations or short work weeks. They need to work long hours to pay for clothes, food, and shelter. But ambitious people with far higher incomes also frequently trap themselves into a Power/Power cycle, telling themselves that they "must" work exceedingly hard.

In fact, many of us are not working hard, necessarily, we're just working all the time. Even when we're not working, we're worrying. There's so much to do! We spend our days, evenings and weekends powering through marketing plans, website upgrades, and professional planning and preparation — then "rush the slide," cheating ourselves of sleep, time with loved ones, and other "recovery" activities that would only enhance our success. By creating a Power/Power lifestyle, we send ourselves in the wrong direction: toward stress, illness, crankiness, muddled thinking.

"Without rest, we respond from a survival mode, where everything we meet assumes a terrifying prominence," writes Wayne Muller in *Sabbath: Restoring the Sacred Rhythm of Rest*. "When we are driving a motorcycle at high speed, even a small stone in the road can be a deadly threat. So when we are moving faster and faster, every encounter, every detail inflates in importance, everything seems more urgent than it really is, and we react with sloppy desperation."[1] Sound familiar?

Rest can mean a "real" vacation, with no business interruptions. It can mean leaving the cell phone home one afternoon and wandering down to your local museum to see an exhibit. It can mean turning off the computer at 6 P.M. and not turning it on again until 9 A.M. (If that sounds extreme, I daresay you need more rest.) It can mean spacious weekends filled with reading, movies, plays, children's activities, religious services, music, photography, or other "recovery" activities that give your mind as well as your muscles a chance to chill out.

If you want your career (and life) to be a marathon, not a short, exhausting sprint, become aware of your own twin needs for exertion and rest. Find ways to establish boundaries around your personal life, so work does not consume you. "When we cease our daily labor, other things — love, friendship, prayer, touching, singing — can be born in the space created by our rest," writes Muller.[2]

Rest: Like power, it's not always easy, it's not always popular, and it requires saying no. Insist on resting, and you might encounter people who tell you you're nuts. But if you want to thrive longterm, rest is as essential as exhaling.

E is for Endurance: Master the Power/Rest cycle.

✳ ✳ ✳ ✳ ✳

TIME OUT FOR REFLECTION

1) Which part of the cycle needs more of your attention: Power or rest? Explain.

_____

_____

2) When do you take time off? What do you say to yourself about that?

_____

_____

3) Have you noticed how much more productive the power phase is when you're fully rested? Explain.

_____

_____

4) When was a time you performed over the long haul and demonstrated endurance?

_____

_____

5) What challenging task are you facing right now? How can you incorporate the Power/Rest cycle so you complete it successfully without compromising your health or relationships?

_____

_____

F is for Forgiveness

Forgive yourself immediately for all mistakes

F is for Forgiveness
The best of us blow it
We miss easy lay-ups.
We need kindness. Show it.

Imagine you're playing basketball. You steal a ball from the other team and dribble furiously down court. Ahead, the basket waits for you, like a promise. It's just there — it's not *moving* or anything — but something goes wrong and you bounce the ball too hard off the glass. It ricochets into the eager hands of an opponent. The crowd groans.

What now? There's no time for self-recrimination. You can't hang your head. You must sprint down court and play defense. If you don't hustle back and play defense, without fouling — if you spend even a fraction of a second acting mad at yourself — then you've made two mistakes. You missed the basket, and you missed the next moments that the game had to offer.

Life is a lot like basketball. It moves very quickly. If you spend even one moment in self-recrimination, you're missing life as it dashes past. This is not to say that we can't notice our mistakes and learn from them. But most of us spend too much time being upset with ourselves.

Instead, do what the athlete must do in the heat of the game: Forgive yourself immediately for all mistakes. Notice the error, adjust if you can, but don't dwell on it. Sprint down court, ready for life's next adventure, whatever that may be.

In basketball, this is called "the transition game": the shift from one end of the floor to the other. Many times throughout a game (after a made shot, a missed shot, or a stolen pass), players find themselves having to dash to the other end of the court, shifting their mindset and behavior from offense to defense or from defense to offense. It's a difficult habit to get into. It's far easier to "get settled" on offense or defense, and expect to stay there a while, then feel surprised and caught off guard when the game shifts. My coach used to have a special whistle she would use during practice to signal "the transition game." When we heard it, we would have to drop (or pick up) the ball and sprint to the other end of the court, regardless of how comfortable we had become with the status quo.

> If you spend even one moment in self-recrimination, you're missing life as it dashes past.

This is what forgiveness requires: a dramatic shift in thinking and positioning. Whether you're forgiving yourself, your teammate, or an opponent, the transition game asks you to let go and move on.

The other night I went out for dinner with a group of friends. They are good friends, so it was a relaxed, safe environment. For some reason I said, "I've got a really funny story to tell you," then I started telling a story that wasn't funny. I rambled on, trying to *make* it funny, but couldn't. As all my friends sat there, looking at me expectantly, waiting for the funny part, I began to feel foolish. Finally I just sort of drooled to a close and said, "That's it, that's all, I'm finished." Being good friends, they started talking about other things. I have no idea *what* they were talking about. I couldn't hear them, because the voice in my head was too loud: "Why did you say that was a funny story? That wasn't a funny story! And why couldn't you *make* it a funny story! What a ninny!"

Then I remembered. As an athlete, I know how to forgive myself immediately for all mistakes. I did so — just saying that line to oneself is often sufficient — and was able to rejoin the conversation.

The relationship between forgiving others and forgiving ourselves

I first learned about self-forgiveness a few years ago, during an agonizing and ultimately liberating process of forgiving the coach who molested me when I was young. During that process I also learned that it is possible to forgive anyone, which led to my writing *The Unburdened Heart: Five Keys to Forgiveness and Freedom*.

The last of my five keys to forgiveness and freedom is self-forgiveness. During my healing process with the coach, I had to forgive myself for having been naive, for having lied to my parents, for not having somehow stopped the abuse. (Sometimes self-forgiveness is required even when you did nothing wrong, or, by virtue of age or innocence, were not responsible for your actions.)

Along the way I noticed how harshly self-critical I am on a daily basis. I learned that when I'm suffering, self-forgiveness is often the answer. Learning from mistakes is essential, but mostly what we need, I believe, is less self-correction and more self-love.

Learning to forgive myself has saved me from endless hours of insomnia. I used to torture myself at night, upset about some small thing I did or failed to do. Not only do I sleep better now, I also forgive others more easily. I'm getting good at that because I practice on myself all the time.

I believe that until we forgive ourselves — for our numerous human failings — we cannot fully forgive others. As long as we are fixated on our own weaknesses, we will remain fixated on the weaknesses of others. As long as we punish ourselves, we tend to punish others. I think there's too much self-flagellation, too much self-loathing. I don't think people need more self-punishment. I think they need more self-compassion.

Doesn't self-forgiveness grant a license to keep misbehaving? Don't we need to punish ourselves for our transgressions to keep ourselves in line? I don't think so. Let's reconsider the basketball player who misses the easy lay-up. If she gets punished — by her coach or herself — the bad shot will remain in her mind, and in her way of thinking about herself. But if she can immediately forgive herself, not dwelling on the failure but instead focusing on the game at hand, she's much more likely to believe in her ability to make the next shot, then make it.

Yet I don't know too many people who treat themselves gently, forgiving themselves for daily mistakes. Often we don't even realize that self-forgiveness would be useful. Instead we berate ourselves, as if brutal self-recrimination might rectify past problems. For many of us, guilt and regret are constant companions.

This internal monologue — I'm sloppy, lazy, incompetent, or worse — only complicates relationships with colleagues, supervisors, and family. Any criticism from them just reinforces what we already know — we're sloppy, lazy, incompetent, or worse — and damages our already fragile self-esteem.

"Throughout life, failure snaps at our heels like a great mongrel dog," said Jackie Gleason. "The key to success is realizing that the dog is really a harmless puppy."

We also tend to blame other people or situations, even for our most personal failures. Late to a meeting, we want to blame the traffic, the snow, or the fact that someone gave us poor directions. Unfortunately, with this type of transgression, it is our fault: for not double-checking the map, for not embarking on the journey sooner. It's the quintessential inside job.

Leadership lessons

When athletes make mistakes, they say to their teammates, "my fault" or (ungrammatically) "my bad." It's a way of taking responsibility, admitting fault — and also acknowledging, in a matter-of-fact way, that mistakes are part of the game.

Many hospitals have institutionalized a frank discussion of mistakes. Physicians and medical students meet weekly for "M and M" (morbidity and mortality) sessions, during which they analyze mistakes that caused illness or death. At mandatory, closed-door sessions, they discuss what went wrong that week and why, in a candid and confidential atmosphere that nevertheless holds guilty parties responsible. When asked, "What could you have done differently?,," the person who erred must respond with some constructive ideas so all can learn from the experience. In this way, the hospital acknowledges two almost paradoxical things: 1) mistakes are unacceptable; and 2) each week, mistakes will happen.[1]

As President of the National Speakers Association/Washington, D.C. Area (NSA-DC), I established a similar ritual. During board meetings, we scheduled time to talk about our recent mistakes.

I initiated this process — which I called "Leadership Lessons" — as

> Susan B. Anthony said, "Failure is impossible!" It was a great rallying cry, but she forgot to say this: Failure is inevitable.

a way to share what I was learning and encourage others to do the same. Over time, it became clear that there were other benefits as well. By not hiding my mistakes, I was modeling self-forgiveness, showing my team 1) that I accepted mistakes as a normal part of life, 2) that I forgave myself for my own, and 3) that I expected them to take risks, make mistakes, take responsibility for those mistakes, and forgive themselves readily as well.

Together, by openly discussing our inevitable failings and what we had learned from them, we created what I have come to think of as a "climate of compassion": a place where everyone felt free to try new things, make mistakes — and relax.

Self-forgiveness is the generous act of giving yourself a break. Remembering that you're human. Offering yourself the loving kindness that you might offer, on your best days, to those you love the most, no matter what they've done. A song says, "Let there be peace on earth . . . and let it begin with me." Self-forgiveness is about "beginning with me." When we "begin with me," we become nicer. We become less defensive. We don't worry so much what others' judgments might be, because we're not judging ourselves.

Susan B. Anthony said, "Failure is impossible!" It was a great rallying cry, but she forgot to say this: Failure is inevitable. Mistakes are part of what happens on the way to success. Those of us who have high expectations tend to be hard on ourselves when we fail to meet those expectations. That's why self-forgiveness is essential.

"Finish each day and be done with it," advised Ralph Waldo Emerson. "You have done what you could; some blunders and absurdities have crept in; forget them as soon as you can. Tomorrow is a new day; you shall begin it serenely and with too high a spirit to be encumbered with your old nonsense."

Failure is inevitable. Forgiveness is what's needed next. Offer kindness to your teammates and friends when they fail — and most importantly, offer kindness to the person who needs it most: the one you live with every moment of the day.

F is for Forgiveness: Forgive yourself immediately for all mistakes.

* * * * *

TIME OUT FOR REFLECTION

1) What, if anything, have you not forgiven yourself for?

_____

_____

2) What would happen if you forgave yourself for all your mistakes?

_____

_____

3) Who do you know who seems to model self-forgiveness?

_____

_____

4) What could you say to yourself the next time you make a mistake?

_____

_____

G is for Goals

Aim high

G is for Goals
Your answers to "Where?"
Without destinations
You'll never get there.

Every time I write a book, my young nephew asks, "How many pages is *this* one, Aunt Mariah?" Chris seems to think my goal is to write the longest book possible. Fortunately for my readers (and for me), I have different goals: to write clear, original, thought-provoking books that entertain, educate, and amuse. Also, because I do this for a living, my books must sell.

Early in my sports career, I learned to define success for myself, setting my own goals rather than letting my success (or failure) be defined by others. People who do not figure this out often drop out of sports. Consider all the second graders who quit Little League because they're "not any good." Or the young kids who stop swimming because "I never win."

Successful athletes often set goals other than winning. Sometimes the goal is to set a personal best, such as running a 10K thirty seconds faster than you ran it last year. Sometimes it's grabbing ten rebounds. Sometimes it's placing in the top ten. For a first-time triathlete, it's often simply finishing the race. Despite America's cultural obsession with gold medals, the most well-rounded and satisfied athletes decide ahead of time how they'll define success, then strive for that.

Whatever their goals, athletes learn to aim high, stretching for an accomplishment that often seems just beyond their reach. In striving for it, they might not accomplish everything they set out to — but they accomplish more than they would have if they had set lower goals.

Marion Jones and striving for five

Remember Marion Jones's goal for the 2000 Olympics? For months leading up to the Games, the track star publicly announced that she planned to win five gold medals. She said this to reporters, to fans, to anyone who would listen: "I plan to win 5 gold medals." Her goal was so high that people began arguing with her. Track and field insiders, especially, were skeptical. They didn't think her long-jump performance was good enough. They didn't think she had the stamina to win all five events. She found herself on the defensive, justifying her goal. Then she refused to talk about it. But she never changed it.

In the Olympics, Marion Jones won three gold medals and two bronze medals. In doing so, she became the first woman to win five medals in a single Olympics. Quite an accomplishment!

> It's not true that "if you believe it, you will achieve it." Believing isn't enough.

She did not achieve her goal. But what if she had not set that five-gold-medal goal in the first place? What if she had agreed with the "experts," who expected less of her? How many medals would Jones have won if she had tried to win just one? What if, like many Olympians, her goal had been simply to *make* the Olympic team?

Here's how many gold medals most of us will win in the Olympics: zero. But in the process of trying to reach our goals, whatever they may be, we learn, achieve, and grow.

Setting goals makes life more fun. A walk on the beach is invigorating and beautiful, but it becomes even more fun, I find, if I set a goal of finding perfect shells or identifying unusual birds. A swim in the ocean makes me feel sensuous and strong, but it becomes even more fun, I find, if I try to catch up to the dolphins frolicking just beyond the breakers. Sure, there is a time for aimlessness — during any ocean swim, I roll over and float on my back for a while, gazing at the glorious sky — but in general, having a goal focuses the attention. As any meditator will tell you, paying attention is more interesting than not paying attention.

The danger of setting low goals

Sometimes athletes short-change themselves by aiming too low. During the US Open tennis tournament in the fall of 2001, my chiropractor, Bill Booker, asked me who would win. "Probably Venus Williams or Jennifer Capriati," I predicted. "I'm not sure. But I do know how Serena Williams will do. She's going to get to the finals, then lose."

"How do you know that?" Bill asked.

"She's been telling reporters: 'My goal is to make the finals.'"

Serena had won the US Open in 1999. So she knew that winning was possible. Yet in 2001, she set a relatively low goal: making it to the finals. Perhaps her confidence was shaken by the fact that her big sister Venus won in 2000. Serena didn't seem to believe she could win the tournament again — and she didn't. Her wish came true. She made it to the finals — then lost to Venus in straight sets.

Six months later, Serena overwhelmed Venus in the finals of the Nasdaq-100 Open, 6-2, 6-2. "This definitely was a milestone for me and for all the younger sisters and brothers out there," Serena said afterward. "It definitely removed a mental block for me."

It's not true that "if you believe it, you will achieve it." Believing isn't enough. There are other necessary elements of success, like hard work. But goals matter. Set them carefully, and be sure to aim high. That way, if you don't achieve that high goal, you'll still achieve a lot. As baseball legend Yogi Berra said, "If you don't know where you are going, you're sure to wind up somewhere else."

Goal-setting in five easy pieces

I use a five-step process for goal-setting:

1) **Focus**: What is your goal? It should be specific and measurable. It should be *yours*: not your father's or spouse's or anyone else's. "I always wanted to be somebody," says "bag lady" Lily Tomlin in Jane Wagner's play, *Search for Signs of Intelligent Life in the Universe*. "Now I see I should have been more specific."

2) **Prize**: What are the benefits of reaching that goal? In other words, what's the prize? By listing the rewards — tangible and intangible — that will come your way, you stay focused on why it's worth the work that will inevitably go into achieving the goal.

3) **Hurdles**: What are the obstacles? How will you run over— or around—them? Anticipating what might go wrong is not negative thinking; it's intelligent preparation.

4) **Game plan**: What's the strategy? Figure out the specific steps you'll take to achieve the goal, including deadlines for completing each task.

5) **Celebration**: How will you keep score and celebrate success? It's important to know when you've "won," and to savor the prize, as well as the experience you've just had. In sports, the scoreboard tells you when it's over. It can be trickier to know in "real life" — unless you decide ahead of time what constitutes victory, and how you'll celebrate success.

Measurement

For goal-setting to be effective, success must be measured. In all the best teams I've observed, the coaches and players keep track of everything — not only in games, but in every practice. Basketball coaches, for instance, monitor layups, free throws, rebounds, and sprint times. Every activity gets recorded and compared, both to past personal performances and to other players. That way, practice situations mimic the intensity, focus, and meaning of game situations, and over time, players can see, appreciate, and celebrate their progress.

The same is true for successful businesses. Everything gets measured: how much money is earned each month, of course, but also such things as how much is spent each month, and on what; how much overtime is paid; how

> I always wanted to be somebody. Now I see I should have been more specific.
> — Jane Wagner, *Search for Signs of Intelligent Life in the Universe*

quickly customers are responded to; how many phone calls are received as a result of a particular marketing campaign; how many employee sick days are taken; how punctual the employees are; how much supplies cost; how many hours or days elapse between taking an order and providing a service; and how many hours employees spend offering community service. Just keeping track of these things requires discipline, but as all business owners know, only that which gets measured improves.

Ask yourself, What could I measure to improve my performance — at school, work, or home? A student can measure much more than grades; she could keep track of the number of hours spent studying, the number of study groups attended, the number of classes attended — anything that might help performance. A spouse who says, "I promise to cook dinner at least once a week" could measure that, writing it down on a calendar on the refrigerator, so he or she becomes accountable to the family. Good intentions — "I'll try to cook more, study more, succeed more" — become achievements when they get specific, and when they get measured.

In any given contest, not everyone can win, no matter how focused they are on their goal, and no matter how well they prepare, mentally and physically. But people who practice goal-setting are more likely to achieve their goals than those who simply dream and hope. Why not be one of the smarter, more successful ones?

"Little girls have told me, 'I want to be like you,'" reports Lisa Leslie, 2001 Women's National Basketball Association MVP. "I tell them, 'Be better than me. Shoot as high as possible. I had high goals. I reached them, and so can you.'"

G is for Goals: Aim high.

* * * * *

TIME OUT FOR REFLECTION

1) What is one goal you have right now?

_____

_____

2) If that goal seems "too high," where or from whom did you get that idea?

_____

_____

3) What action steps are you taking to achieve that goal?

_____

_____

4) Describe a time when you "aimed high" and achieved a goal. How did that feel?

_____

_____

H is for Humility

Ask for help

H is for Humility
Help!'s tough to say.
But keep in mind: Teammates
Feel needed this way.

"HELP!" That's what basketball players say when they're on defense and the person they're guarding flashes past. When all goes well, teammates take over, picking up where the hapless defender left off.

As a coach, I've had to coax players to do this: to yell, loudly, "HELP!" It's a public plea for assistance — and, for some, an embarrassing admission of inadequacy — but it's an essential part of the game. It's also a key ingredient in team success, on or off the playing fields.

What's it like in your workplace? Do people openly seek the help they want or need? Do they acknowledge and work to improve their weaknesses?

What's it like in your personal life? Do you ask your spouse or other family members for help?

Humility can be harder than it sounds — especially when you're seen as successful, or need to see yourself as successful for your own self-esteem. Admitting that you need help — whether in the form of assistance, answers, attention, or just more practice — can feel risky, as linguist Deborah Tannen noted in her famous obser-

Do people in your workplace openly seek the help they want or need?

vation that men are often reluctant to ask for directions. She's right. Some men do fear that asking for directions might make them appear incompetent. Women in male-dominated professions can feel the same way. Sometimes, to ask for help is to admit that one is lost, literally or figuratively.

Yet through vulnerability comes strength. When the player yells, "Help!" he often receives exactly what he needs — and thus strengthens himself and the team.

"We are all struggling," wrote Kabir, a 15th-century Sufi poet. "None of us has gone far. Let your arrogance go and take a look inside."

"Coachable"

As a center, I spent many hours practicing my dribbling. Practicing shooting was more fun, but because I was not naturally good at dribbling, I wanted to at least strive for adequacy. I was not expected to dribble much on the court (mostly, in those days, a center would receive a pass, turn, and shoot) but I became persuaded to practice my dribbling the hard way: by having the ball stolen from me by small, sneaky guards. Sometimes humility is preceded by humiliation.

Dotty McCrea, my Stanford coach, used to commend me for being "very coachable." I didn't understand, then, why anyone would *not* be coachable. Isn't it in our best interests to listen to those who know more, and learn everything we can from them?

But in the intervening years, I've met many people who are not coachable, and have seen that tendency in myself. Sometimes I don't feel open to criticism, constructive or otherwise. I'm too defensive about some behavior or trait — or too attached to a perception of myself as knowledgeable, successful, or "together" — to readily accept advice or feedback. Like asking for directions, receiving critical feedback can make one feel weak, but in fact, it requires and builds character.

I've been speaking professionally since 1987, but didn't learn about the National Speakers Association[1] until about 1994, when a speaker named Lou Hampton gave a presentation for Washington Independent Writers, another association of which I was a member. After hearing his speech, I told Lou, "I'm interested in joining the National Speakers Association — not to improve my presentation skills, just to get more business."

"Why wouldn't you be interested in improving your presentation skills too?" he asked gently.

Oh. Whoops! Of course I would and should be interested in improving my presentation skills — no matter how talented or experienced I might be. I've since found out that that's one of the many joys of NSA membership. There's an ethic of humility, hard work, and generosity as members continually strive together to improve all aspects of our "game."

Success is built on continuous, lifelong learning. Successful people are constantly seeking knowledge, about themselves and the world. They're humble, they're curious, they're open to what each activity might teach them. After an achievement, they reflect on what went well. After a disappointment or loss, they bring that same humility to the experience, assessing what happened and learning all they can.

Humility is an athletic essential. Listen to your mentors, colleagues, friends, and even foes — the "coaches," "teammates," "fans," and "opponents" — who can help you improve. Listen to your own body, too, seeking insights about nutrition, strength, flexibility, and rest. Be open-minded and humble enough to learn continually from others, and from your own inner wisdom. Set an example for colleagues and friends by asking for help, and by addressing the weakest parts of your "game."

> We are all struggling.
> None of us has gone far.
> Let your arrogance go
> and take a look inside.
> — Kabir

H is for Humility: Ask for help.

* * * * *

TIME OUT FOR REFLECTION

1) When's the last time you said, "I need help"? Describe the situation, including how you felt about asking, and how people responded.

   _____

   _____

2) When's the last time you said, "I need you"? What happened as a result?

   _____

   _____

3) What's the weakest part of your "game"? Could you humble yourself and ask for help in developing this part of your personal or professional life? Whom will you seek out to help you improve?

   _____

   _____

I is for Integrity

Play the ball as it lies

I is for Integrity
Follow the rules.
Play the ball as it lies.
Cheating's for fools.

If you play golf, you have probably noticed that many golfers cheat. You might not include yourself in that category, and you might not consider the following behaviors cheating, but unless players have specifically agreed to play by "winter rules" or "beginner's rules" or their own original rules, all of these activities are against the rules:

- Moving a ball with a foot or club to improve its position
- Treating each hole's final putt, no matter how long, as a "gimme"
- Counting a score of 8 as a 7
- Capping the score on any hole at double par, or 6, 7, or 8, even if one actually shot a 10 or 12
- "Fudging" the final score or the handicap
- Taking "mulligans"

I've never encountered this phenomenon in other sports, perhaps because even at the amateur level, other sports are more likely to have referees or umpires, whose job it is to enforce the rules. Some unscrupulous tennis players try to gain advantage by calling a ball out when it's in, and some athletes in other sports inflate their statistics and attempt to cheat now and then, but I can think of no sport in which cheating is so commonplace, pervasive, and accepted, as golf. When a recreational golfer hears another golfer say, "I'll give myself a six," the listener is not surprised by this, takes no particular note of this, and fully understands that "six" is not the actual score, but the ego-saving score the inventor finds sufficiently tolerable to write down.

Playing by the rules, pure and simple

By contrast, professional golfers, for whom fame and fortune might rest on whether a score is or is not a six, take the honor system seriously, and periodically penalize themselves for mistakes that no one else witnessed. Wendy Ward, for example, gave herself a penalty stroke in the McDonalds's LPGA championship in 2001 when her ball rolled infinitesimally after she addressed a ten-foot putt. No one saw her touch it and television cameras could not detect any movement, but she knew the ball "resettled on the green" because, she explained, she always lifted the ball to mark it while her partners putted, then replaced it on the green with the logo facing the same way, and she saw that the ball was not the way she had placed it. Therefore she must take responsibility.

> Golf provides excellent opportunities to practice humility, honesty, and even courage in the face of subtle pressures to cheat. So does life.

When reporters questioned her about this afterward, she was, like other golfers who have similarly penalized themselves, very matter-of-fact. "There's not much of a story on that," she said. "Golf is a sport of integrity and honesty. We play by the rules, plain and simple."

Yet amateurs tend to distort the rules, and the score, to their advantage. I understand the temptation. Golf is a notoriously impossible game, only made more frustrating by the accurate tallying of the score. As far as I can tell, the score always seems like it "should" be lower than it actually is.

When I started playing about ten years ago, I observed this pattern and made a decision not to cheat — partly because I'm interested in how much I might improve over time, and the only way to determine that is to create a meaningful measurement device, i.e., a "real" score, and partly because long ago I made a conscious decision to live a truthful life.

I don't mean to sound self-righteous. The fact that I do not cheat in golf does not make me a good person, nor a better person that those who do. Amateur golfers are free to keep score in whatever way they please. But I do find that golf provides excellent opportunities to practice humility, honesty, and even courage in the face of subtle pressures to cheat.

So does life. We all face challenges that test, then strengthen or weaken, our integrity, along with our self-esteem. We all face crossroads where we can choose honesty or dishonesty. None of us make perfect or perfectly consistent choices. And most of us, I would conjecture, find it difficult to "play the ball as it lies" — to accept life exactly as it occurs, resisting all temptations to "improve the lie" with small adjustments that we hope no one will notice.

Cheating is commonplace

We all know of commonplace situations in which cheating is accepted, even expected. Consider how often people joke about cheating on their taxes or brag about ways they do. Recall friends' stories of lying to police officers to avoid receiving tickets. There's a winking sort of complicity in this widespread phenomenon, even among people who believe themselves to be honest.

Consider the question, "What shall we say to Mom about being late?" Or, "What shall we tell Jennifer so we don't have to go to her party?" Friends and families often construct fictional stories for each other. Ostensibly this is done with the intent of saving someone else's feelings — but that, too, may be part of the fiction: that it's better to lie and "not hurt her feelings" than to tell the truth and potentially deepen the intimacy.

What if we said, "We're late, Mom, because we got in an argument on the way here and sat in the car for a while to reach some resolution before coming inside. It's embarrassing, because it seems grown siblings should not still be squabbling"? Or, "I'd rather not attend your party, Jennifer, because I recently quit drinking alcohol, and I'm uncomfortable around people who drink"? Couldn't these honest confessions actually improve relationships more than the invented tales so many of us tell?

Integrity is defined by my dictionary as 1) the firm adherence to a code of moral values; 2) incorruptibility; 3) the quality or state of being complete or undivided; and 4) completeness. It comes from the word integrated, meaning whole, and it seems to me that we can't really separate one aspect of our lives — the "I misrepresent my golf scores but really it's no big deal" part — from other aspects, like whether we tell the truth to friends, spouses, or the government.

Can cheating at golf (or anything else) become a slippery slope, leading to other forms of cheating? Of course it can. When you lie to yourself or your partners, you get in the habit of lying, and that habit is bound to be expressed elsewhere.

Even if people "compartmentalize," cheating at golf but not cheating themselves or others in other domains, such inconsistencies can damage one's own sense of integrity. That "little white lie" — "I shot a 90" — is bound to affect one's internal sense of self, at least in some minor way.

Success should not be measured only in terms of quantifiable results. "For when the One Great Scorer comes to write against your name — He marks not that you won or lost — but how you played the game," wrote sportswriter Grantland Rice. Success should be measured by tallying up all aspects of "playing the game," including the final score, one's enjoyment of the day, the beauty of the surroundings, the camaraderie of one's partners, the joy of hitting the ball well (even if that's infrequent) — and one's integrity.

"Golf is not everything," says Tiger Woods. "It never will be. The most important thing is furthering yourself, making yourself a better person."

Perhaps this is the difference between amateurs and pro's, on and off the golf course. The amateurs cut corners, creatively keep score, engage in "little white lying" to themselves and others. Pro's like Wendy Ward — and most successful leaders and achievers — "play by the rules, plain and simple."

Playing by the rules is not always plain or simple. It can be a daily challenge to be honest, to be ethical, to do the right thing. Few of us adhere firmly to a strict code of moral values. But athletes would do better to follow the example of the pro's. After all, isn't life, like golf, a game of "integrity and honesty"?

I is for Integrity: Play the ball as it lies.

* * * * *

TIME OUT FOR REFLECTION

1) Describe the moral or ethical code you live by.

_____

_____

2) How do you feel when you're at a crossroads, deciding whether or not to tell the truth?

_____

_____

3) Name someone in your life who has integrity. How do they demonstrate that?

_____

_____

J is for Joy

Raise the roof!

J is for Joy
Kids don't need advice
But grownups: Please don't
Let "contentment" suffice.

"When you're happy and you know it clap your hands
Clap Clap
"When you're happy and you know it clap your hands
Clap Clap
"When you're happy and you know it and you really
want to show it
"When you're happy and you know it clap your hands
Clap Clap"

If you were a parent waiting as the Shady Grove Junior High School bus pulled into the parking lot after an "away" game, you could never tell whether the kids on that bus had won or lost the game. My teammates and I would sing en route to other schools, then play the game, then — regardless of the final score — we'd sing on the way back. Always, through the open bus windows, parents could hear the happy sounds of teenage girls singing songs, clapping hands, stomping feet, and laughing.

In high school, things changed. The first time we lost a field hockey game and began singing on the way home, our coach stood, glared at us, and angrily announced that there would be no singing after a loss. Chastising us, she insisted we contemplate our defeat in silence the entire 45-minute ride home. Respecting and even fearing her, we complied.

I remember how surprised I was, and uncomprehending. Were we being punished? I had never before been punished for losing an athletic competition. Were we being taught a lesson? If so, what was the lesson?

That coach was a good coach, and her intentions were no doubt good as well. She probably wanted us to take sports seriously, believing in a positive correlation between seriousness and success. She probably wanted us to take losing seriously, believing that unrestrained happiness after a loss would lead to more losing. Disappointed about our performance and wanting us to feel the same way, she probably equated post-defeat singing as a sign that we didn't care, or didn't care enough.

Here's where she was wrong: We did care. We cared about practicing, we cared about playing games, and most importantly we cared about and enjoyed each other so much that whenever we were together, we sang. Such team spirit should be cultivated. By insisting that we silently lament losing on the way home, she was interfering with our natural *joie de vivre* — a key ingredient in any and all success.

Unfortunately, that coach was typical of coaches, leaders, managers, and grownups in general. Many of us mistakenly equate maturity with solemnity, and overlook or even squelch the simple human need for joyful expression. As we grow increasingly self-conscious about and embarrassed by defeat, we downgrade our natural joy to mere "contentment" or "satisfaction."

Who stops to savor success?

Adults often stop celebrating success, too. Especially among ambitious people, there's a tendency to rush forward to the next goal, the next achievement, without pausing to savor the glory of success.

Sports offer many pleasures and benefits, but their initial and most obvious offering is this: they're fun. This is why children seek athletic challenges. It's fun to run, throw, and catch. It's fun to accomplish something with your body, with your teammates, with nature. The best athletes continue to experience this joy, and allow it to radiate from their pores, even as the stakes rise. "I like to run with fun in my heart," explained Australian Cathy Freeman after winning the 400 meters in the 2000 Olympics.

"Sometimes the water goes so fast beneath you it seems it will tear your wetsuit right off," says bodysurfer Lauren Crux. "You can feel the whole ocean rushing along your belly. Nothing matters — work, outside pressures — everything goes away, and all that's left is a sense of peace. It's a profound, relaxed, deeply erotic, and sensual feeling. When I step out of the ocean, I've been transformed."

Watch a basketball player after he makes an important or impressive bucket. As he runs down court he'll steal a moment to smile, to nod or point to the person who passed him the ball, to high-five another teammate, to chest-bump his pal, or to "raise the roof," pushing the palms of his hands up toward the ceiling in a proud gesture that says, "We are so hot we're blowing the roof off this place!"

> I like to run with fun in my heart.
> — Cathy Freeman,
> Australian Olympic champion

Now imagine the manager who completes a deal or "scores" by conducting an efficient and productive meeting. Where's the high-fiving? Who raises the roof? Who even exchanges nods or smiles with this person as he or she walks through the halls on the way to the next event on that day's calendar?

Why not raise the roof in the workplace? It's a dramatic, contagious, and playful gesture of obvious celebration. As every athlete knows, how we move our bodies affects how we feel about ourselves and the world around us.

> Work like you don't need the money.
> Love like you've never been hurt.
> Dance like nobody's watching.
>
> — baseball champion Satchel Paige

Celebrations matter. They honor the natural human spirit of joy, regardless of the arena and regardless of the magnitude of the accomplishment. Even small victories deserve recognition. An atmosphere of frequent celebration boosts morale.

"You will be judged most not by the work you do but by the love you put into your work," said Mother Teresa. Yet most people work so hard, and with such stress and serious intent, they find it easy to overlook the love part — and the joy. Who has time to celebrate? Deadlines loom.

In my mastermind group, we begin our meetings by listing our recent accomplishments, thanks to one of our members, Lynne Waymon, who has gently insisted on these ritual celebrations. This has become an integral part of each meeting, so we don't succumb to the temptation to focus all our attention on problem-solving. Because it's structured, no one feels shy about celebrating their latest successes. We have created a culture of celebration, and it sets a tone of joy, gratitude, and optimism for the entire meeting.

Joy and laughter at work

Madelyn Jennings, former senior vice president for personnel for Gannett Company, says joy was a secret of her leadership success. "At staff meetings we had a lot of laughter because afterward you're more creative," she explains. "Also because it's fun to laugh."

Her advice to people dealing with workplace pressures: "Don't lose your sense of how funny the whole thing is. Often, in meetings, when faced with the most serious business matters, some CEO will say, 'Just remember, it's all a game.' They're not being irresponsible. Somehow when you view it that way, you go at it in a stronger fashion, with more creativity and more concern for your colleagues."

Barbara Kay Carlson, an internal communications specialist at Chicago's University HealthSystem Consortium, has integrated joyful celebrations into the structure of employees' days. Employees fill out forms called Caught in the Act (CIA) of excellent customer service, reporting each other's good work. One copy goes to the boss, one goes to Carlson, and at monthly "celebrations and appreciations" meetings, all CIA recipients are applauded, while a few are randomly selected to receive small prizes.

About ten percent of the employees "resisted at first," complaining that it was a waste of time, Carlson admits. "Changing a culture is not an easy task." But the celebratory atmosphere is now so appealing that temporary workers often comment on how positive and enthusiastic everyone seems.

The difference between bronze medalist Michelle Kwan and gold medalist Sarah Hughes at the 2002 Olympic Games was joy. While Michelle wobbled, fell, and tried too hard, Sarah expressed the exuberance of the young and unafraid. The same thing had happened four years earlier, when Tara Lipinski's happiness overwhelmed Kwan's careful attempt to win. Judges don't give points for *joie de vivre* per se. Nor do supervisors or bosses. But when joy radiates from one's soul, it can't help but make one more attractive and successful.

Joy is about abandonment: letting go of traditional social constraints and allowing yourself to celebrate. "Work like you don't need the money," advised baseball champion Satchel Paige. "Love like you've never been hurt. Dance like nobody's watching." That's joyful abandon.

J is for Joy: Raise the roof.

* * * * *

TIME OUT FOR REFLECTION

1) Describe a time when you felt joyfully alive.

2) What is something specific you accomplished lately — large or small? How did you take time to enjoy your achievement?

3) How are you planning to celebrate other successes?

4) Who will share in the fun?

K is for Knowledge

Develop your physical intelligence

K is for Knowledge
The physical kind
Your body speaks louder
Than even your mind.

All day long, your body talks to you, offering a minute-by-minute report on its needs, joys, and problems. Using the language of pain, pleasure, yearning, sensation, and stiffness, your body says twelve basic things:

1) I'm hungry.
2) I'm thirsty.
3) I'm satisfied.
4) I'm tired.
5) I'm sore, sick, or injured.
6) I'm happy.
7) I'm emotionally upset.
8) I need to be touched.
9) I need to be alone.
10) I need to use the bathroom.
11) I need to move.
12) I need to stretch.

Your relationship with your body is the most central and enduring relationship of your life. What sort of relationship is it? How do you two get along? When your body talks to you, what do you say in response? When your body gives you information, what do you do with that? Are you supplying your body with what it needs to perform at its peak?

Self-knowledge is not something one can acquire, then check off a list. It requires an ongoing process of listening and responding because the body changes all the time. It's difficult to respond wisely and appropriately because we often have other priorities — making money, taking care of other people, getting from here to there — that can take precedence over what our bodies would like us to do. It's difficult because we live in a culture in which we're encouraged to pay more attention to our body's outward appearance than to its intrinsic health. It's difficult because of conflicting messages and desires. The tongue might say, "Feed me carrot cake" while the stomach says, "I'm already full from dinner." And it's difficult because it's not just a physical and intellectual process, this communication between body and brain. We also have feelings about our bodies' needs and desires. We might feel guilty or disappointed. We might grieve our loss of agility or ability. We might feel victimized, responding defensively, "I *shouldn't* be injured or ill! I *was* taking care of myself!"

> Your relationship with your body is the most central and enduring relationship of your life.

Here are three primary ways people respond to physical messages:

1) Denial,

2) Misguided attention, and

3) Conscious attention.

For example: "I'm hungry."

1) Denial: "I'm too busy to stop working right now."

2) Misguided attention: "Here's a Snickers bar; that will do."

3) Conscious attention: "Gee, what sort of food am I hungry for? What does my body really need? What will give me nutrients and energy? I'll go eat that, and only that."

Your body is talking to you, desperately trying to communicate its needs. Who else can it talk to? Only physicians, if it comes to that. And it will, if you fail to do your job. Eventually your body will end up in a physician's office or emergency room, and there it will plead its case with someone else, still searching for a sympathetic ear. At that point, healing will be harder. It's easier to keep the body functioning smoothly when you have listened all along to its needs for food, water, rest, exercise, and love.

Please don't feel guilty about not taking care of yourself perfectly. No one does. Developing physical intelligence takes practice and patience. No one can offer a body the conscious attention it wants all the time — any more than a parent can offer a child all the attention it wants all the time. So moments of clear, conscious attention will invariably be interspersed with moments of misguided attention and moments of denial. This is natural. Our bodies are not perfect, and nor are our attempts to take care of them.

Please be easy on yourself when you mistakenly ignore the body's signals. There's an expression in golf — "Don't follow a poor shot with a stupid one." In other words, if you hit the ball into the woods (poor shot), don't try to weave your next shot through sixteen trees (stupid). Instead, take the safer, wiser route out of trouble, back onto the fairway.

So too with physical intelligence. If you eat too much (poor shot), don't vomit that food into the toilet (stupid) or starve yourself for the rest of the day (stupid). Just get back onto the course of your life, recommit yourself to paying conscious attention, and proceed.

For some of us, paying attention is a totally new concept. A woman named Brenda started walking at age 38, training for a three-day, 60-mile walk to raise money for cancer research. Wanting to successfully complete the walk, she asked me a series of questions about shoes, socks, stretching, pacing, drinking, eating, and mileage per day. She posed her questions in terms of my experience, such as, "Do you drink Gatorade?" so at first I answered them that way. Eventually I realized that she was looking for information and guidance entirely outside of her own experience. Regardless of whether I drink Gatorade, it might work for her. Regardless of whether I wear Nikes, those might be the best shoes for her. Finally I explained that her body will tell her what it needs. "It's fine to ask experienced athletes for their advice," I said, "but your body is unique, and what works for you will not be identical to what works for anyone else." This notion — that her body would tell her what's right — was foreign to her, and surprising. With no athletic experience, she was not in the habit of listening to her body. Of all the benefits she gains from this three-day walk, beginning to develop self-knowledge (and self-trust) might be the most significant.

A knee story

My knees have been talking to me for a long time. In college, they began to shout, expressing their anguish and pain. But I was a basketball star, and loving every minute of it — not the stardom so much as the experience itself, the incredible joy of playing the game and playing it well. Sure, my knees were talking to me, but knees are very small and far from the willful brain. How trivial knees can seem when an athlete hooks a ball up and over an opponent in a perfect arch. How inconsequential those patellar pains become when four teammates are depending on the fifth to drive hard to the bucket, then ease the ball gently through the hoop. My finely tuned body brought me incredible pleasure. Finely tuned teams magnified that pleasure to the point of ecstasy.

When my knees' cries of pain became too loud to ignore, I consulted a doctor, who warned, "The strain you're putting on your knees now may cause you to develop arthritis by the time you're forty." At twenty, forty was light years away and arthritis was no more imaginable than cataracts. So I proceeded to rebound, dribble, pass, and shoot for several more years, and in that process did irreparable damage (severe chondromalacia) to both knees.

Now my knees and I have a deal (bargaining is an integral part of the grieving process, as Elisabeth Kubler-Ross noted): If I don't run, jump, or pivot, and if I lift weights three times a week in order to sustain quadricep strength, and if I

> **Physical fitness affects how you do everything, and how you feel about everything you do.**

stretch religiously, I can enjoy what I have come to think of as the "sitting and floating" sports (cycling, rowing, swimming), and can also walk (including on golf courses) without pain.

But I still must listen and respond on a daily basis — not only to my knees, but to my shoulders (two surgeries so far) and to the rest of this complicated package of ambition and limitation. I don't claim to have mastered this athletic essential. I can only testify to its importance, since I've struggled with it all my life. I have a high pain tolerance, apparently, as many athletes do. In the heat of a competition, I'd much rather sprint than slow down, regardless of what my joints have to say on the subject. Racing around the Washington, D.C. mall on my bike, I can still get so caught up in the beauty of a cool breeze and a pleasant "burn" in my thighs that I forget to pay attention to my little tiny knees and their little tiny needs. So I'm constantly learning, learning, learning — and forgiving myself (see "F is for Forgiveness") when I make the wrong choices.

I do feel fortunate to be learning these lessons now, before old age. Some people live relatively pain-free until hospitalized late in life for some drastic illness or injury. At that point they feel betrayed by their body. It must be harder, it seems to me, to start listening *then*. Whereas I already have considerable experience with pain and loss. I know that even if we eat healthy foods, stretch and strengthen our muscles, do "all the right things," our bodies will still disintegrate over time. That is their nature. This is sad, of course, but only makes me more grateful for each day of health, vitality, and agility. It's this deep gratitude that I find most helpful, and that I remind myself to tap into when I'm frustrated with my limitations. Curiosity can also help. What can I learn from this experience? How can I use this to improve my relationship with my body — and my overall fitness — over time?

Athletes develop physical intelligence

Ideally, athletes become physically intelligent: knowledgeable about the body's needs and desires. Athletes respond wisely and compassionately to the body's requests, gently helping the body become stronger, happier, fitter, more flexible.

"Really great athletes baby their bodies," says Olympic swimming champion Nancy Hogshead. "You grow up with the axiom 'No pain, no gain,' but it does not apply. You push yourself right up to the point where your body wears out, but you never cross over that point. Rather than seeing your soul and your body as two separate things, you have to be teammates. The body is full of wisdom, and so is the mind. You have to get over the finish line together."

Your body is talking to you. But it's not a one-way street. You are talking to your body, too. You might praise it. You might appreciate it. Or you might be disrespectful, insulting, or downright verbally (or even physically) abusive. We talk to our bodies through our thoughts and beliefs, some of which will occasionally be articulated to others, as in, "I hate my body," or "I'm so fat," or "I'm terrible at sports." These statements have tremendous power.

A landmark study in the early 1990s showed that women who believed they were prone to heart disease were nearly four times as likely to die as women with similar risk factors who were not so pessimistic. The pessimism itself, apparently, triggered death. They literally "worried to death." The study has been validated by other studies, including several showing that people who are warned about a medicine's side effects are much more likely to experience those side effects.[1]

This is called the "nocebo" effect. It's the opposite of the placebo effect, in which an improvement in health status results from one's faith in a pill or other treatment that is ostensibly impotent. With the nocebo effect, it's a negative belief (such as "I don't want to live" or "I am not strong enough to survive this") that becomes the self-fulfilling prophesy.

With this in mind, consider the potential effects of these thoughts on one's well-being:

- I've always been uncoordinated.
- I don't have much energy.
- I'm the ugly one in my family.
- My thighs are disgusting.
- I catch colds easily.
- I have no control over my eating.
- I'm accident-prone.

From nocebo research, it seems logical to conclude that the body will respond *somehow* to these messages from the mind. Exactly how will vary from person to person. One way or another, negative thoughts can actually program people for bodily failure.

As we develop physical intelligence, we learn to listen not only to the signals the body gives us, but to the thoughts we have about our bodies. Both — our bodies and our thoughts about our bodies — need conscious, loving attention.

This is part of what it means to be an athlete: you respect your body. You take care of it. You find some way to exercise that works for you, and you do it until it becomes a daily discipline. You do it until you enjoy it, then you keep doing it, even on the days when you don't enjoy it so much. You do it because you're an athlete, and that's what athletes do. And you do it because physical fitness affects how you do everything, and how you feel about everything you do.

Athletes say kind things about their bodies, treating their bodies like cherished, lifelong partners. Athletes make a momentous commitment to their bodies, promising to have and to hold them, from this day forward, in sickness and in health.

K is for Knowledge: Develop your physical intelligence.

* * * * *

TIME OUT FOR REFLECTION

1) What has your body told you so far today?

_____

_____

2) What have you said to or about your body so far today?

_____

_____

3) What's one specific way you'd like to respond to something your body has been telling you lately?

_____

_____

4) What's one negative thought or feeling you have about your body that you could frame more positively?

_____

_____

5) What percent of the time are you honest with yourself about what your body is trying to tell you?

_____

_____

L is for Leadership

Be the kind of person who's worth looking up to

L is for Leadership
Not how, but who?
Are you a good person
Worth looking up to?

I first became aware that I was a leader one day at sixth-grade recess. We had just sprinted from the classrooms onto the grassy fields. I found myself surrounded by a giggle of girls, all jumping up and down, raising their hands, and shouting to me:

"Can we play dodge ball?"

"Can we play baseball?"

"Can we play kickball?"

I thought, I'm not the teacher. Why are they asking me?

Maybe it had something to do with the fact that they were literally looking up to me. Or maybe it was because I already "stood out" as an athlete. When you're an athlete, people look up to you. People are naturally drawn to those who seem courageous, confident, and competent. Despite Charles Barkley's infamous, "I am not a role model" comment, athletes — even young ones — become role models. A role model is one who leads by example, whether they're aware of that leadership role or not.

"In influencing others, example is not the main thing; it is the only thing," said the philosopher Albert Schweitzer.

I carefully considered what to do. Should we play dodge ball — my favorite? Should we play baseball, because Laurie liked baseball, and I liked Laurie, and I wanted her to invite me to her birthday party?

Or should we play kickball — which is what we usually played — because it was the easiest for everyone?

I don't remember what game I chose. I do remember that I tried to be fair and inclusive. I tried to make sure everyone had a good time. And I did choose. I said, "Okay, here's what we'll do." I accepted the mantle of leadership.

You never know who's looking up to you

That day on the playground, I learned a major life lesson: you never know who might be looking up to you. I made a major life decision: to become the kind of person who is worth looking up to, just in case anyone's looking. I decided to be fair, to be kind, to be a responsible citizen in my family and in my grade-school community. I didn't always succeed — as Ben Franklin famously discovered, perfecting one's own character traits can be difficult at best — but the intent had been formed, along with the commitment.

> In influencing others, example is not the main thing; it is the only thing.
> — Albert Schweitzer

Later, as captain and leading scorer of the Stanford basketball team, I tried to bring hope and enthusiasm to the team each day. I was the one saying, when another team took the lead, "That's okay, we can catch up." I was the one leading the celebrations when we won. And I was the one talking to the coach when other players were unhappy about her decisions. Understanding that my teammates were looking to me for leadership increased my sense of authority, and gave me a chance to consciously exercise leadership skills.

Now, as an author and professional speaker, I'm aware that some people look up to me, and I still take that responsibility seriously. Over time, I've developed what I think of as an athletic approach to leadership, based on the principles of relationship, responsibility, and integrity.

Leadership as relationship

Leadership used to mean sanctioned power or authority. Leaders were kings, presidents, popes, politicians, coaches, and executives who had been granted the term "leader" by virtue of their position, and who ruled over their "subordinates." In the past twenty or thirty years, experts have changed the way they think about leadership. They have begun to appreciate the fact that anyone can lead, that people can lead in a variety of ways, and that the best leaders often employ a collaborative, empowering style, rather than one based on authority and top-down directives. Nowadays leadership development programs teach people to build trust through listening, honesty, empathy, authenticity, accessibility, and a team orientation. Even the United States Navy advocates what they call "covenant leadership," founded on the values of honor, courage, and commitment.

Management guru Peter Drucker defines "leader" in its most simple terms: "Someone with followers." But even people in a designated leadership role become followers from time to time, and vice versa. Susan Devereaux, a competitive ballroom dancer and also my executive assistant, taught me this when I asked her about the woman's role in ballroom dance.

"We use the terms followers and leaders, not women and men," explained Devereaux, who began ballroom dancing at age 44 as a social activity. Seven years later, she competes and performs regularly on a Pro-Am basis, and recently won 22 out of 23 dances she entered in a local ballroom "dancesport" competition.

"Actually both people play both roles, especially as you become more accomplished. You're constantly adjusting. It would be inconsiderate of me to expect my partner to always be on.

Sometimes, to accommodate the conditions on the dance floor or for a different interpretation of the music, I decide to change a step and just pick up the ball and run with it."

The same is true in our relationship, Devereaux pointed out. "In my work for you, I might be following up on a lead you have given me, but during the course of that phone conversation I might hear something, and I'll want to go with it, and not let it drop by the wayside just because it wasn't in my instructions. Sometimes I need to take the initiative and see where something goes, rather than coming back to you and asking for direction all the time."

Ballroom dancing offers a wonderful opportunity to learn about leading and following, Devereaux says. "You learn to let go and let someone else be in charge, setting the general path that you're moving toward. But you also recognize that there are times when it's beneficial for you to take charge — not in a risky way that would upset the apple cart, but in a way that would add a new dimension to the dance." The reverse is also true. "Not only does the follower have to learn to be a leader, the leader has to learn to be a follower."

Leadership as responsibility

What those girls on the playground were really asking for when they encircled me with raised hands was this: "Will you be our leader?" The invitation came from others. The decision to say "yes" was my own.

I could have said no. I could have said, "I really don't know which game is best. You decide." We've all met people like that. Even when offered choices, they resist making decisions.

"Which restaurant do you prefer?"

"Oh, it doesn't matter to me."

"Which direction shall we take with this project?"

"Oh, I don't care."

"What kind of wedding shall we have?"

"Whatever you want is okay."

There's not necessarily anything wrong with abdication of responsibility, though it can be annoying and ineffectual. It's just not what leaders do. Good leaders are willing to make decisions, for themselves and for others. They're willing to step up, state their opinions, express their views, and negotiate for what they want. It's not coercion. It's a confident assertion of one's own rights and responsibilities.

I know a Zen Buddhist teacher and author named Cheri Huber. Cheri and her students sometimes venture beyond the monastery — to shop for food, to visit a restaurant, to deliver toys and other gifts to children. I have accompanied Cheri on these outings, and was at first surprised that even when she runs routine errands around town, she wears her long black robes. One time I asked her, "Why do you dress in your robes, even when you're not teaching"?

"There are two reasons," she said carefully. "I want to be accountable. And I want to be accessible."

As often happens during conversations with Zen monks, she did not elaborate. But for me, these became defining qualities of leadership: accountability and accessibility. If you're accountable, you accept personal responsibility for your actions, regardless of whether anyone else happens to be watching. If you're accessible, others can readily identify you as a leader and learn from you, directly or indirectly.

Leadership as integrity

One of the leadership models I find most useful was designed by Lolma Olson, founder and president of Sage Consulting, a company based in Northern California that serves primarily the health care industry.[1] Olson's model, Heads, Hearts, Hands,™ offers a unique way of analyzing and assisting organizations and individuals. It's deceptively simple, eminently practical, and based on a physical analogy that athletes can easily relate to.

Like athletes, leaders must commit to excellence with every fiber of their being. Using their heads (thinking clearly, planning, making good decisions) is not enough. Opening their hearts (caring, connecting, relating) is not enough. Using their hands (working hard, modeling impeccable ethical behavior, accomplishing tasks, following through) is not enough.

Successful leaders, Olson says, implement all three: Heads, Hearts, and Hands. Integration and balance are key. Employees in successful organizations — like individuals in healthy bodies — are able to think, feel, and achieve, without ignoring or short-changing any of the three.

But organizations — like the individuals who work there — tend to get out of balance, resulting in poor productivity, low morale, and poor management-employee relations. Most often forgotten are the Hearts, says Olson. "We're good at embracing projects but we haven't put as much effort into embracing people: the personal relationship side of things. We tend to be afraid it would be messy or emotional. Or we're not in touch with our own feelings. Or we're simply moving too fast to listen or talk or celebrate. So we leave out the Hearts."

Hearts are the feeling part: feeling empathetic, compassionate, and alive with enthusiasm and excitement. An organization that does well in the Hearts department is one in which people feel cared about, respected, included, and recognized. They smile. They talk to each other. They know why they work. They know that their opinions count.

Not surprisingly, Olson is an athlete. She's a former tennis player, race-car driver, and trapeze performer who now hikes and studies and teaches T'ai Chi — which best exemplifies the role of Heads, Hearts, Hands™ in her own life. After practicing T'ai Chi, Olson says, "My head is clear, my heart is open, and my hands are ready to receive and give what they need to."

How can business, association, government, or student leaders employ the Heads, Hearts, Hands™ concept? Here's one example: At NSA-DC, I instituted a Heads, Hearts, Hands™ process in our board meetings. I crafted clay sculptures of a head, a heart, and a hand, and brought them to each meeting, asking for volunteers to take responsibility for each of these three aspects of our process.

The "heads" person asked us periodically: Are we making a wise decision? Are we thinking this through clearly enough? The "hearts" person spoke up if she or he sensed interpersonal tension between board members, tried to make sure people felt included and appreciated, and reminded us to take time to applaud each other's work. The "hands" person reminded us about action items: What follow-up needs to happen? Who will write an article for the newsletter? What's the deadline for completing this project?

Thinking, feeling, and doing should be shared responsibilities in any group, but I found it helpful to name these three priorities in the beginning of each meeting, and to have the visual symbols sitting there on the table with us. Like many new ideas, mine was not embraced immediately or wholeheartedly. My colleagues teased me about the sculptures, calling one (accurately) "the ugliest heart in the world." But the model soon became a working part of our vocabulary, as any of us would say: "We need some more Heads work on this one," or "What's the Hand part of this decision?" or "We need to pay more attention to our Hearts." It helped us integrate the three essential parts of any project: thinking, feeling, and doing.

> We need to explore ways to be powerful and persuasive while also being responsive and respectful.

Reluctance to lead

Some women aren't comfortable with leadership. They don't want anyone looking up to them. They want everyone to be equal. Gloria Steinem was recently asked by a caller on a radio show, "Which women do you look up to?" She recommended that, rather than looking up to each other, women should look across to each other. From this position of equality, she asserted, we can all learn from and respect each other, regardless of the skills, talents or experiences any of us bring to the table.

I'm all for equality, and I respect Gloria Steinem. In fact, I look up to her for her thoughtfulness, her clear writing, her willingness to lead a diverse and changing movement over several decades. I think it's okay to look up to other women. I think it's okay for men to look up to women too, and for women to look up to men. You can look up to others without feeling "less-than," without damaging your own deep sense of worth. You can admire, respect, and learn from teachers, athletes, coaches, parents, therapists, spiritual leaders, and other role models without feeling smaller or weaker or inferior. In fact, it's a sign of strength to humble yourself enough to look up to others.

Some men aren't comfortable with leadership because they learned about leadership in the old school, which taught that leaders are people who have power over others, and use it in any way they please. These men have bad memories of being bossed around, and try not to act bossy themselves. But a man who leads without a certain bossiness can be considered feminine or weak. And a man (or woman) who leads through dominance or intimidation meets resistance, because most adults (and children) resist being told what to do.

Both women and men would benefit from detaching leadership from gender roles altogether. We all need to explore ways to be powerful and persuasive while also being responsive and respectful. We all need to remember that, whether or not we're in a position of authority, others are looking to us for guidance, assistance, inspiration — in other words, leadership.

As athletes, we need to ask ourselves, What sort of role models are we? What sort of leaders do we want to be? How should we take responsibility? What sort of relationships shall we have with our teammates, colleagues, peers? How can we become accessible and accountable? How can we integrate Heads, Hearts, Hands™? How can we become the kind of people worth looking up to, in case anyone's looking?

L is for Leadership: Be the kind of person who's worth looking up to.

* * * * *

TIME OUT FOR REFLECTION

1) Do you think of yourself as a leader? If not, what would have to change in order for you to do that? How would that affect your behavior and self-image?

_____

_____

2) Who looks up to you?

_____

_____

3) Of Heads, Hearts, and Hands, is there one you tend to overlook in your work or personal life? Explain.

_____

_____

M is for
Mental Game

See yourself succeeding

M is for Mental Game
The clear inner sight
To see yourself winning
To know your path's right.

Dorothy Harris was a pioneering sports psychologist from the University of Pennsylvania who, toward the end of her life, had a unique opportunity to practice her own preaching. Suffering from cancer, she decided to use her powers of visualization to prevent hair loss, despite undergoing chemotherapy treatments that usually cause baldness. Each night she visualized retaining her full head of hair, and each morning her friends and family marveled at her thick hair — and the powers of her mind. Then one day she woke up, looked in the mirror, and realized something was amiss. Her hair still looked good, and a few gentle tugs reassured her that all was well. But something else was missing. Finally she saw it. "My eyebrows are gone! Oh, darn! I forgot to visualize saving my eyebrows!"

Visualization — the ability to "see" and hence create success — is one of the hallmarks of sports psychology. Studies have shown that basketball players who just practice free throws, for instance, are not as successful as those who practice free throws and also spend time sitting quietly, imagining themselves shooting (and making) free throws.

At its most effective, this mental rehearsal process includes not only visualization — not just "seeing" the result — but also imagery: hearing, smelling, tasting, and touching success. The athlete who is mentally rehearsing doesn't just "watch" the ball go in the basket, she also "listens" to the sounds of the fans; "smells" the scents of the gym; "touches" the ball with her fingertips; and "feels" her knees bend, her muscles contract, her arms and hands shoot and release the ball as it spins toward the basket.

"For every movement, there is a set of expectations generated, against which the ultimate movement is contrasted," explains University of Virginia psychology professor Linda Bunker, Ph.D. "Before you swing a golf club, for example, you set up some 'expected sensory consequences' (how it will feel, sound, look), and then you evaluate the product against those expectations.

"If you let those expectations run in your mind before you swing, you get a 'mulligan' — that is, you can subjectively match your motor plan against how you hope it will work. Then after 'checking it out' you can actually swing."

The same would be true for anticipating any event: a job interview, an important meeting, a tricky task. Imagining it in advance gives your mind as well as your muscles time to rehearse. See yourself sitting up straight, looking people in the eye, thinking clearly. Imagine feeling confident, relaxed, alert. Hear the sounds you might hear in that situation. Bring the entire event to life in your mind. That way, by the time you get there, you will have already "been there," in a sense. Even though you won't be able to imagine all the possibilities, you'll get a "feel" for how things will go, and thus things will more likely go your way.

Everything is beautiful in its own way

Another mental strategy athletes use is interpreting virtually everything in a positive light. Rowers will say to each other, "We lost the race, but we were faster than last year." Bowlers will say, "I got fewer strikes than I wanted, but I did well converting those spares." Coaches talk about "building years," "stepping stones," "setting the stage for the future." Athletes buoy their own spirits by reminding themselves of past successes, quietly patting themselves on the back. Even when they lack confidence, they manufacture it by engaging in what's called "positive self-talk," creating a running internal monologue of encouragement.

"Often you can look at a player or a team and see what happens when the confidence level shifts and they begin to lose the mental game," observes Michael Hylton, who has competed nationally and internationally at the highest levels of wheelchair basketball, softball, and tennis. "It can be dramatic, and can prove to be the difference between victory and defeat. Conversely, having a positive, optimistic outlook toward the outcome of the game — even in dire circumstances — translates into more confident and relaxed play, enabling one to overcome difficulties.

"Likewise in relationships. The positive expectation that the "right" results will come about allows each party to relax and be more candid, which leads to honest dialogue and an optimum outcome."

> Ninety percent of sports are mental. The other fifty percent is physical.
>
> — Yogi Berra

If you listen, even for a moment, to the kinds of things you say to yourself and others throughout any given day, you'll begin to get a sense of how positive or negative your own mental game may be. Do you criticize yourself or others as not good enough, not witty enough, not smart enough, not attractive enough? Do you expect success or failure? Listen to your thoughts. They will tell you how you perceive the world and what sort of attitude you bring to each experience.

Attitude is a decision. It's a choice you make: Do you approach the world with gratitude and optimism? Do you see (and hear and feel) yourself as successful? Do you expect positive outcomes? Do you speak to yourself with kindness and compassion?

Like most other things, a positive attitude can improve with practice. When you fail to live up to your own expectations, try saying, "I can make it next time" or "Nice effort" or, very gently, "What can I learn from this?"

Athletes also train their minds to focus on the task at hand, despite distractions. They even practice hitting balls or doing cartwheels while coaches or teammates deliberately try to distract them. It's this acquired ability to calmly concentrate that stands them in good stead down the home stretch, whether it's for Olympic gold or a regional Little League title.

> You can tell a lot by how a player talks to, and listens to, her parents.
>
> — Pat Head Summitt

The inimitable baseball legend Yogi Berra once said, "Ninety percent of sports are mental. The other fifty percent is physical." He was right, in a sense. People who say "it's all in your head" are exaggerating; athletes (and others) need physical skills and tremendous physical strength, stamina, and flexibility to achieve great things. They need to practice shooting free throws in the gym with real basketballs. They can't just imagine practicing. But without the "ninety percent" that is mental, no athlete — or coach, teacher, doctor, musician, financial planner, or chef — will sustain a long, successful career.

Mind over matter

In a recent survey of 658 coaches from 43 different sports, athletes' psychological attributes were overwhelmingly rated as the most important underpinning of success. The coaches, who work with males and females ages 3 through 22, were asked to "describe a young athlete who is a real winner" by picking 5 attributes from a checklist that included 64 physical and 64 psychological characteristics. The most frequently mentioned characteristics were all psychological: "loves to play" (43%); "positive attitude" (33%); "coachable" (30%); "self-motivated" (28%); and "team player." (26%). Others in the top 10: "strives to improve" (21%); "dedicated" (21%); "gives best effort always" (19%); "good sportsmanship" (16%); and "encourages/praises others" (15%).

No physical characteristics were even mentioned in the top 10. The first was #19 overall, and it was selected by just 10 percent of coaches: "natural physical athlete." "Physically pushes self" was 20th; "good hand-eye coordination" was 21st.[1]

Recently I observed a Washington Mystics pre-season practice while the coaches were deciding which players to keep and which to cut. There I had the opportunity to ask some of the country's top coaches to answer a similar question. First I posed the question to Mystics head coach Marianne Stanley, who coached Old Dominion University to three national championship titles and won another two as a player, at Immaculata College.

"What's the most important quality you look for in a player?"

"Competitiveness," she said without hesitation. "They can have tremendous talent, but if they don't want to do anything with it, if they don't want to win, if they don't want to work hard to improve, the talent will be wasted."

Next I asked Pat Head Summitt, who has coached the University of Tennessee to six national titles. Summitt serves as player personnel consultant for the Mystics. "Nowadays what I look for is character," she replied. "Do they have good values? Do they respect themselves and other people? I watch how they talk to their parents. You can tell a lot by how a player talks to, and listens to, her parents. How unselfish are they, on and off the court? We're looking at the top players in the country, but within that pool, I'd say it's character that determines which ones will fit into our team, our family."

Linda Hill-MacDonald is the Mystics' assistant coach. What does she look for in a player? "Attitude. Willingness to work hard. I'd rather have a player with less talent and good attitude than a player with more talent and bad attitude. They should always be wanting to get better."

Jody Lavin-Patrick, the women's basketball coach at Flint Hill School in Oakton, Virginia, was also attending the game. Lavin-Patrick chairs the Potomac Valley AAU program, a basketball program that involves 6000 teen and pre-teen girls, so she sees a lot of young people. "What I need is focus," she said. "There are so many distractions these days. Kids have unbelievable schedules. I need kids who will look me in the eye, listen, hear what I'm saying, and do their best to do it. If they give me that kind of focus, I can develop their talent. But if they're too distracted, they'll never be good."

Are psychological characteristics such as "loves to play," "positive attitude," "coachable," "self-motivated," "competitive," "respectful," and "focus" just as important for artists, plumbers, web designers, managers, government workers, sales representatives, physicians, professors, accountants? Of course. Skills count too — you can't be a scientist if you don't know science — but it's the mental game that, in the "real world" as well as in sports, is essential if you want to spell success.

M is for Mental Game: See yourself succeeding.

* * * * *

TIME OUT FOR REFLECTION

1) When you rehearse an important event in your mind, is your image positive or negative? Explain.

_____

_____

2) What kinds of things do you say to yourself when mentally preparing for a game, interview, or presentation?

_____

_____

3) Do you positively interpret losses or disappointments? Give an example.

_____

_____

N is for Nagdeo

May you have experiences that lead to good dreaming

*N is for Nagdeo
What does that mean?
Play hard but play gently
So you'll have good dreams.*

In *The Kin of Ata Are Waiting For You*, Dorothy Bryant depicts an unusual and utopic society in which people make daily decisions based on what they dreamed the night before. In greeting, they say to each other, "Nagdeo," which means "May you have experiences that lead to good dreaming."

The book became a cult classic in the seventies, when lots of young people were following their dreams, literally and figuratively. I used to go backpacking in Yosemite, and named my igloo-style green tent "Nagdeo Turtle." It was a playful gesture, but also a reflection of the fact that I took "Nagdeo" seriously.

> **Drinking and taking drugs do not lead to good dreaming.**

I used to ask myself and my friends: Which experiences lead to good dreaming? Which do not? Backpacking produced good sleep, we noticed, which led to good dreaming. Same for basketball, volleyball, swimming, aikido, judo, and all other forms of physical exercise. Reading, writing, and other artistic expression produced stimulating thoughts and images, which led to good dreaming. Friendships, massage, and other loving touch produced good feelings, which led to good dreaming. The very act of paying attention to dreams, we discovered, also led to good dreaming.

Caffeine, alcohol, and other drugs did not lead to good dreaming. Staying up late did not. Worrying did not. Anger did not. Jealousy did not. TV did not. Once we decided to seek experiences that led to good dreaming, life's choices became clear.

What I was really asking was, Which of my actions will have positive results? It's an important connection for a young person to make: that every action has consequences. Buddhists call this karma.

Athletes follow their dreams. They commit themselves to achieving their dreams. They believe that dreams matter. They believe that actions have consequences. They learn to differentiate actions that will help them achieve their dreams from actions that will not. And while pursuing experiences that lead to good dreaming, they notice that dreaming leads to more good experiences.

An Olympic dream

In 1975, when I was a sophomore at Stanford, I learned that women's basketball would make its Olympic debut in 1976. Before that, it had never occurred to me to play Olympic basketball, because the opportunity did not exist. But suddenly I had a new dream, and a new question: Which experiences will lead me to fulfilling my Olympic dream?

Fortunately, two teachers appeared to help me. One was Ken Morgan, a Stanford coach who graciously and generously volunteered to assist me with physical training: running, weight lifting, ball handling, shooting, defensive drills. I was already in good shape, but Ken reminded me that the best players in the country would attend this try-out, and that I must become even more fit. He established a rigorous six-day weekly workout schedule that got me in the best shape of my life.

Once I committed to this training, it became imperative that I decline numerous invitations to do the things many other college students were doing: drinking, taking drugs, staying out late, partying in the dorms until dawn. None of this would lead to good (Olympic) dreaming.

A vegetarian and "health food freak" since high school, I further refined my diet, eliminating all sugar. I was also careful to stretch my muscles, get enough sleep, and spend time each day in mental rehearsal, imagining my dream coming true.

My friends, for the most part, did not understand. How many 19-year-olds turn down social invitations so they can go to bed early? How many refuse alcohol — and even ice cream and cake — at their own birthday parties? Explaining that I was in training for the Olympic trials didn't help much, since in those days there was little understanding of women's commitment to sports. Like many pioneers, I felt lonely but at the same time clear about the importance of disciplining myself to do everything possible to reach my dream.

> Athletes learn to differentiate actions that will help them achieve their dreams from actions that will not.

In fact, as a teenager, I probably could have handled a scoop of pralines and cream here and there — or one late night with friends — without any negative effects on my physical conditioning. But making a total commitment helped me keep my focus. And by the time I reached Reno, Nevada, the site of the trials, I felt confident that I had done everything I could to prepare.

My other teacher was a sports psychiatrist named Jim Gough. He taught me how to meditate, how to use bio-feedback to lower my heart rate, and how to visualize athletic success. He also taught me how to set boundaries. In basketball you have to say "no" with your body: grabbing a ball away from someone who wants it, defending your position with a wide stance and expressive elbows, stepping in front of someone to block their path. Like many girls, I had been raised to be "nice" — and lacked requisite aggressiveness on the court. Dr. Gough gave me permission to take up space, to claim the court as my own, to refuse to let people push me around. He taught me that in order to say "yes" to any dream, you have to say "no" loud and clear to whatever might jeopardize the dream — not only drugs, alcohol, and toxic foods, but also people who try to get in your way. It was an important lesson for me, one that I've put to use in many ways throughout the years, especially when people try to "push me around" off the court.

I did not make the 1976 Olympic team. As a 19-year-old sophomore, I just didn't quite rate as one of the top twelve players in the country. Three years later, when my skills were at their peak, I chose to turn pro (in those days, Olympians were amateurs) instead of waiting a year to try out for the 1980 team. That turned out to be a good decision, since Americans boycotted that year. By 1984, I had retired.

So I never became an Olympian, but in the process of setting my sights there, I learned a lot: how to focus on a goal, get in shape, improve my skills, avoid distractions, visualize success, choose foods that enhance performance, and stand my ground. I also learned how to compete against the best players in the country. The Olympic training improved my game, which led to my playing for a French professional team and for the New Jersey Gems of the Women's Basketball League. Although I did not achieve my original goal, my experiences did lead to other good dreams and other rewarding accomplishments.

N is for Nagdeo: May you have experiences that lead to good dreaming.

* * * * *

Time Out for Reflection

1) What do you currently dream of doing or accomplishing?

_____

_____

2) What's a current experience that leads to good dreaming for you?

_____

_____

3) What people or events get in the way? Have you had the clarity to say no to the temptations that could derail your dream? Explain.

_____

_____

O is for Opponents

See opponents as opportunities

O is for Opponents
Shake hands. Say "Great game."
Without them, your skill level
Would stay the same.

If you think of yourself as an athlete; if you're focused, forgiving, and joyful; if you're competitive, humble, and disciplined; if you aim high to achieve your goals; you will have opponents. Opponents are people who get in your way — if you let them. But if approached with the right attitude, they can help strengthen your resolve and teach you new skills. Often, without meaning to, they can even help you.

One of my first opponents was the boys' high school basketball coach at Arcadia High School in Phoenix, Arizona. The year was 1972. There was no girls' team.

I had just moved to Phoenix. I knew how to play basketball, and had excelled at it in the Philadelphia area, where they offered teams for girls starting in seventh grade. By the time I moved across the country with my family, I was 16 years old, about 6 feet tall, and had already played high school varsity ball for two years. But none of the Phoenix schools had girls' teams. So I approached the boys' coach, who was also my astronomy teacher. At six-four, he was the only teacher taller than I. Summoning my courage and pulling myself up to my full height, I proclaimed, "I'd like to try out for your basketball team." It was not a question.

He laughed. I shrank a little but persisted. "I played at my old school," I said. "I'm good."

"You can't," he said.

"Why not?" I asked.

"Your breasts would get in the way," he said.

I took a step back.

"Your breasts could get hit with an elbow," he said, demonstrating the risk by pointing his elbow at my chest, then extending it so it stopped just inches from my blouse.

I took another step back. "Just let me try out," I persisted.

"Only if I can personally bind your breasts," he said with a smirk.

The term sexual harassment had not yet been coined. I don't think I even told my parents. I just didn't try out. The boys' basketball coach defeated me — but not for long. I was already an athlete: competitive, confident, committed to achieving my goals. So, without asking their permission, I joined a boys' intramural team, sprinting up and down court with the boys who weren't quite good enough to make the varsity. A few refused to guard me, afraid I'd embarrass them, but most accepted me, treating me like "one of the guys."

> You've been diagnosed with an incurable disease? Oh happy blessed opportunity!

More importantly, my gym teacher, Sandy Haddock, noticed and invited me to try out for her women's team, the AAU Phoenix Dusters. I did, and quickly joined the starting lineup. My teammates were in their twenties and thirties. We traveled around the southwest, winning the Arizona State Championship twice and competing in the AAU National Championships. That experience helped me gain the attention of Stanford University. My Stanford success led me to the pro's, and to a career as a sportswriter and professional speaker.

So in a sense, I won. The high school basketball coach's opposition kept me from achieving my immediate goal but didn't ultimately defeat me. It probably strengthened my resolve.

How opponents can help

You can only shoot baskets by yourself in your driveway for so long. Eventually, you need some company: someone who plays with you, challenging you to shoot over them, dribble around them, outwit them. Because of this opposition, you improve. That's why you welcome them and thank them afterward. They challenge you to develop new strengths and skills.

This attitude of gratitude for opposition is more difficult to cultivate at work. Opponents can be harder to spot there, and harder to deal with. Our tendency is to waste energy resenting them, disliking them, or trying to change them. But if you think like an athlete, you begin to welcome opposition because it can challenge you in helpful ways, forcing you to become wiser, more flexible, more committed to achieving your goals.

Matt Rogan, a high school student and soccer referee, saw an opponent as an opportunity at a recent soccer game, and thus "won" in a situation in which others might have lost, or at least lost their heads. Before an upcoming game, Matt received a call from the referee supervisor, who places referees at particular games. The supervisor warned Matt that one of the two coaches Matt would be working with was notoriously quick-tempered, and that this coach's behavior toward other teenaged referees had bordered on abuse. County officials would be present, Matt was assured, but Matt's boss just wanted Matt to be prepared.

So Matt prepared. "I'm looking forward to it," he told his mother after the phone call. "I'll have to ref a perfect game."

On game day, the sidelines were quiet through the first half, and again through the second half. Matt felt disappointed. Apparently the troublesome coach had not attended the game. Afterward Matt asked his boss about it. "Oh, that coach was here," the supervisor explained. "He just couldn't find any fault with you, because you reffed a perfect game."

Happy blessed opportunities

Zen teacher Cheri Huber, when faced with a difficult situation, responds with, "Oh, happy blessed opportunity!" It's one of five Zen "gratitudes." Among Zen students, the phrase is used ironically, often accompanied by great laughter, in response to crises. Your car breaks down in the middle of rush hour traffic? Oh happy blessed opportunity! You've been diagnosed with an incurable disease? Oh happy blessed opportunity!

The humor comes from the reluctant recognition of this truth: Difficult situations *do* offer opportunities to learn, to develop patience or endurance, to rise above a human tendency to wallow in the mud of self-pity. They offer opportunities to awaken, as Buddhists put it, to that particular moment and all it has to offer.

It's a useful paradigm. Rivalries offer opportunities to assess goals, get in touch with feelings, and deepen relationships. Your best friend applies for the same job as you? You're turned down for a promotion? Your spouse has been acting jealous ever since you started fulfilling your lifelong passion to study art? Oh, happy blessed opportunities!

Maybe you suffer because of a colleague's bad judgment or bad manners. Maybe your teenager stays out all night. Maybe you're discriminated against at work. Okay, so now what? Are you going to let any of these things defeat you?

"Obstacles are what you see when you take your eyes off the goal," some say, and it's a nice adage, but the truth is, we've got to see those obstacles too. A hurdler may have her eye on the end of the track, but if she can't see the hurdles with her peripheral vision, she's not going to jump over them. At the same time, in order to pace herself properly, she does have to focus on the finish line. It's not either/or. She sees both.

Opponents are a lot like hurdles: you have to go around them, but in the process of going around them, you develop a lot of useful skills, like how to run and jump at the same time.

The perfect retort

Do you know how sometimes you think of the perfect retort — days or even years after you meet an opponent? It took me more than a decade to think of a response to that boys' basketball coach at Arcadia High. But in 1985, I wrote a play called

Out of Bounds, which takes place in a locker room right after a women's basketball team has won the national college championship. In the play, a reporter asks one of the athletes some of the questions I used to get asked all the time:

- "Do you have a boyfriend?"
- "Do the men in your life approve of your playing basketball?"
- "Isn't basketball unfeminine?"
- "Isn't there a conflict between being a woman and being a basketball player?"

The reporter also asks this question:

- "Don't your breasts get in the way?"

The character named Rita finally replies, "Well, yes, George, every once in a while, I do have a problem. Every once in a while, when I'm dribbling down court, the ball bounces up and gets caught in my vagina."

The play has been produced in eight cities in the U.S. and Canada, and of course I've watched some of these productions, so I've had the pleasure of listening to audiences laugh at my script. That line of Rita's is one of the funniest I've ever written — in part because of

> Opponents are not always people. They can be our own habits, beliefs, fears, and insecurities.

the surprising use of the taboo word, of course, but also because Rita creates a graphic image that matches the absurdity of the reporter's questions. There's nothing more gratifying for a writer than hearing an audience laugh at her jokes. Maybe I'll write that boys' basketball coach a thank-you note!

The toughest opponent

Opponents are not always people. They can be our own habits, beliefs, fears, and insecurities. In fact, the one opponent many people struggle with the most is the one inside, the one who says, "You're not good enough, smart enough, pretty enough, thin enough, successful enough, rich enough…" whatever. This opponent can also become an opportunity, but he or she requires special handling, and special attention. (See "F is for Forgiveness.")

O is for Opponents: See opponents as opportunities.

* * * * *

TIME OUT FOR REFLECTION

1) Who is an opponent you're dealing with right now?

_____

_____

2) Could you see this person as an opportunity to become stronger and more resolved? Explain.

_____

_____

3) Can you think of a time when an opponent defeated you? What happened?

_____

_____

4) Think of a time when you avoided a situation because you didn't want to deal with opponents. How could you handle that situation now?

_____

_____

5) What might you say to yourself the next time a rival challenges you?

_____

_____

P is for Purpose

Where is your heart's true home?

P is for Purpose
What do you need?
Where are you going?
Nurture that seed.

I live in Arlington, Virginia, just a few miles from the Pentagon. Like many Americans, I experienced the September 11, 2001 attacks as "hitting home." For weeks afterward, I felt depressed, anxious, deeply sad — and astonished, trying to comprehend the incomprehensible. While Reagan National Airport remained closed, I slept fitfully to the sound of F-15 and F-16 fighter jets circling overhead. I wondered, Why did the hijackers kill themselves and thousands of other people? How should America respond? What would the terrorists do next? Who began sending anthrax through the mail? I couldn't tap into any spiritual perspective that would ameliorate my grief and anxiety.

I regained my equilibrium only when I re-focused on my own reason for being. *What is my purpose?* I asked myself... and I remembered my mission statement: "To demonstrate courage, compassion, creativity, excellence, and humor as I write and speak the truth as I understand it." As a writer and speaker, I can continue to do that. I don't have to resolve or even fully com-

> A mission statement helps you clarify where your song comes from.

prehend a complex international conflict. I can donate money, I can pray, I can stay informed, I can vote, I can bake brownies and walk them over to the Arlington Fire Department, but mostly I need to focus on who I am, and pursue my own path.

A mission statement is a succinct, memorable description of your purpose — in life, at work, in school, or in sports. Broader and deeper than a goal, which is specific and time-sensitive, a mission statement reminds you who you are. It can also help shape who you are, as you commit yourself to following that path.

Roberta Flack was once asked, "What makes a great singer?"

"You've got to know where your song comes from," she replied.

A mission statement helps you clarify where your song comes from.

Here's a mission statement from a man who took a workshop with me: "To alleviate suffering of children by providing foster parenting and encouraging others to do so."

Here are a few more:

"To create a healing environment in my hospital and my home."

"To inspire seniors to greater health and happiness by organizing a softball league for men over 70."

"To have a positive impact on everyone I see when I walk out my front door each morning."

The heart's true home

I wrote my mission statement in my thirties, and it remains true for me in my forties. If I had written it in my teens or twenties, it probably would have included words like "heal" or "change." I used to think it was my job to fix people, and the world in general. I don't anymore. When I assessed what my purpose is, I clarified that I'm a nonfiction writer and speaker — hence the part about writing and speaking "the truth as I understand it" — and that I feel compelled to "demonstrate courage, compassion, creativity, excellence, and humor," verbally and nonverbally, in public and in private.

If I do those things well, others might be inspired, motivated, challenged, and perhaps changed. But I don't need to change, heal, or fix them. And, despite the chaos and even war around me, I don't need to be a politician or diplomat or soldier or judge. I just need to be myself.

The Spanish word *querencia* is defined as "affection," "longing," or "favorite spot." I've also heard it translated as "the heart's true home."[1] I ask myself this as well: *"Where is my heart's true home?"* Just asking that question points me toward peace.

> They must answer, in unison: "To make ourselves better people."

Coaches give pep talks. They ask, "Do you want to win?" They assert, "The team that wins is the team that wants it more." Sometimes that's true. But desire can't be generated from without. It has to come from within. It comes from knowing who you are and what you want and what your purpose is. Usually, when you define your purpose, it's not winning. It's something deeper and more lasting.

Why are we doing this?

Bill Finney is head women's basketball coach at Marymount University (in Arlington, Virginia), one of the nation's best Division III programs. He reminds his athletes of their purpose every day. Known for his grueling workouts, Finney insists that his players execute drills with precision. He watches as they shoot, dribble, rebound, and sprint until they're gasping for breath. But the team's immediate goals — getting in shape, winning games — are not his only focus. While they're panting, sweating, and struggling through pushups or wind sprints, Finney asks his players, "Why are we doing this?"

They must answer, in unison: "To make ourselves better people." Not better basketball players: Better people. Finney wants to win games, of course, and does. But he works his players hard because hard work, goal-setting, and teamwork are character-building activities in themselves. That's his mission: to make his players better people. It becomes his players' mission as well.

Some people believe the terrorist attacks of September 11 have made Americans better people. We seemed to remember our higher values, at least in the short term. Greed was out; generosity was in. Commercialism was out; consideration was in. In the Washington, D.C. area for a few months afterwards, road rage disappeared entirely. In ordinary places like grocery stores and street corners, people treated each other with obvious respect and restraint, acutely aware that all of us had been injured, and that any passerby might be suffering from the ragged torment of new grief.

Of course, that's always true. Any stranger you meet might be suffering horribly. The day terrorism hit home, we remembered that. The day terrorism horrified us and confused us, some of us began to ask the big questions that we should be asking anyway: What is our heart's desire? Why do we work hard? What will we do with this incredible gift we have been given: our lives?

P is for Purpose: Where is your heart's true home?

* * * * *

TIME OUT FOR REFLECTION

1) When do you feel most at peace?

_____

_____

2) When do you feel most satisfied?

_____

_____

3) In one or two brief and memorable phrases, what is your personal or professional purpose? Start with "To," then use a verb, such as build, communicate, connect, counsel, create, discover, educate, embrace, encourage, explore, facilitate, foster, gather, generate, give, heal, hold, improve, inspire, involve, know, lead, live, love, make, master, measure, model, participate, perform, persuade, play, practice, prepare, produce, promote, provide, pursue, relax, reclaim, reduce, reflect, reform, remember, respect, restore, return, safeguard, satisfy, save, sell, serve, share, speak, support, take, team, touch, trade, translate, travel, understand, use, validate, value, verbalize, volunteer, work, worship, write.[2] Then, after you've chosen a verb or two that best fits your purpose, answer: for whom or what? And under what circumstances? You'll then have a mission statement in roughly this format: To [do] [something, for or with someone] [under these circumstances.]

_____

_____

_____

_____

_____

Q is for Quitting

Choosing not to play can be a victory

Q is for Quitters
Truth is, they do win.
Everyone must stop
Sometime. It's no sin.

My friend Wilhelmina Swenholt and I saw *Any Given Sunday*. We expected the movie to be about football but mostly it's about how difficult it can be to respect your own body when the team and coach and culture want you to ignore your broken back or concussion or herniated disk.

"Suck it up," says the coach, played by Al Pacino.

Willie and I did a lot of sucking it up when we played college basketball. We've got four sore knees to prove it. The movie was on the second floor of the theater, and afterward we limped downstairs, leaning on the railing. We laughed, but it's really not too hilarious to be permanently disabled as a result of playing basketball.

Like many athletes, I have a long history of sprains, fractures, dislocations, and surgeries. Like many athletes, I heard the phrase "quitters never win" and believed it. Like many athletes, I kept playing long after I should have quit.

I sprained my first ankle at eleven. My foot got caught between my bike's frame and the wheel. Swelled like a blowfish. Required crutches. Fascinated me.

I remember the squishy swelling, the ace bandage that left its imprint in my skin. The pain was not so much agonizing as interesting. Negotiating stairs on crutches became another athletic feat. The wooden crutches themselves intrigued me, with their removable rubber padding for hands and armpits. The crutches could be adjusted if I turned their tiny silver wing nuts, so I could lower them and lend them to shorter friends. Or I could leave them adjusted for me and let friends pole vault down the school halls while I sat, leg propped up, laughing. The crutches became a status symbol, a tomboy's trophy, proof: I'm an athlete.

> You can quit and still be a winner. You'll just win a different game.

But what's cool to a kid can become problematic as a teenager and young adult. As my injuries multiplied, I began a multi-year regimen of weight-lifting, ultrasound, tape, ice, and heat. I approached physical therapy as another game at which I could excel. And kept playing.

One Halloween, my housemate dressed up as me. I was amused by the sight of Sheila in my Stanford basketball uniform but when I saw the two bags filled with cotton balls, representing ice, I realized that injury had become part of my identity, an integral part of my athleticism.

Playing in pain

So, too, with many employees, supervisors, executives. Listen to people brag about their 12-hour days or 60-hour weeks and you can hear echoes of the supposedly brave athlete "sucking it up" and playing in pain. These people pride themselves not on accomplishing tasks so much as working so hard they bruise themselves along the way. Their trophies are not crutches but dollars, awards, fame, or other proof of their hard work. Addiction to work becomes part of their identity, and quitting seems inconceivable.

"Quitters never win and winners never quit" makes sense when you're twelve and need the motivation to stay on the team even though you hate wind sprints. It makes less sense when you're an adult, able to weigh the pro's and con's of a situation but unable to do what's right because of old myths about quitting.

Tammi Blackstone played basketball at Drake University in the late nineties despite her congenitally misaligned kneecaps. "It's basically bone on bone," she told *USA Today*. She received injections of synthetic cartilage. She wore a brace. She did physical therapy. She applied ice. She had surgery. The pain got worse. Walking hurt. She kept playing basketball.

"She goes through the pain for us," said her teammate Haley Sames.

Is that a good reason to grind bone on bone?

"I also want to be a good role model," said Tammi. "I don't want kids to see me quit just because my knees are bad."

Tammi's choice was hers to make (and I made a similar one), but in retrospect, quitting because one's knees are bad makes a lot of sense. It makes a lot more sense than "sucking it up." A quitter could provide excellent role-modeling for other kids who are facing the same difficult choices. A quitter could say, in effect, "This is my body, and I'm going to cherish it above all other commitments to my team and my school."

Persistence is laudable. When persistence can help you obtain your goals without injuring yourself or others in the process, persist away. But if you're sacrificing your health — or the health or welfare of your children, elderly parents, or other responsibilities — in the name of obtaining those goals, please reconsider. If you're persisting even though the situation seems unethical or unprofessional or just not right, please reconsider. If you're persisting even though the demands on you are unreasonable, please reconsider. And if you're persisting just for the sake of persisting, with little or no chance of success, please remember: It's okay to quit. You can quit and still be a winner. You'll just win a different game.

> You have a right to question your current path.

Becca Carter quit playing basketball in eighth grade, after she tore the cartilage in her right knee. As a young woman, Becca now competes in surfing tournaments. Her knee still "aches, swells, grinds, crunches, and pops," she says. Surfing is "almost as hard on knees as basketball," she admits. But what she learned from her early knee injury, she says, "is to listen to my body. It's a good thing to push yourself, and sometimes you need to play when you're a little bit hurt. But it's also good to learn when to call it quits."

Mountain climber John Roskelley, commenting on those who have failed to reach the summit of Mount Everest, said, "You've got to know when to turn around."

Quitting anything — a sport, a job, a relationship — can be excruciating. But not quitting can be even more painful in the long run. Those of us who refuse to quit when we should — whether we continue "playing" in athletic arenas or business settings or bad marriages — can hurt ourselves: our bodies, our integrity, our chances for future happiness and success. We also hurt others: the loved ones we might ignore because we're too fixated on victory; the rivals we might cheat because winning becomes the only thing; the potential teammates we might alienate when we push onward blindly, in the wrong times and places. The truth is, choosing to quit can be a victory in itself.

Quitter's Bill of Rights

Here's my Quitter's Bill of Rights:

- You have a right to question your current path.
- You have a right to decide you don't have what it takes.
- You have a right to quit.
- You have a right to mourn the loss of your dream.
- You have a right to hold your head high, even if family members or others express disappointment or disapproval.
- You have a right to change your mind.
- You have a right to try again.

Quitting can mean you're wise enough to respect your body, your health, yourself. It can mean that you've outgrown a childhood game, or a grownup job. It can mean that you're ready for new adventures, that you need new stimulation, or simply that you've changed and the old activity doesn't suit you anymore.

Q is for Quitting: Choosing not to play can be a victory.

* * * * *

TIME OUT FOR REFLECTION

1) Have you had good experiences with deciding to quit? Explain.

_____

_____

2) Can you think of a current activity that you might want to consider quitting? What is it?

_____

_____

3) What would it say about you if you chose not to do something that is wrong for you?

_____

_____

R is for Rebound

Persist in the face of disappointment and defeat

R is for Rebound
Then rebound some more
Rebounds, not missed shots
Determine the score.

Life is a game, sure. Life is fun, precious, beautiful, holy. Life is also heartbreaking and terrifying and depressing and extremely disappointing.

Enter the art of rebounding. To rebound is to recover from a mistake, misfortune, setback, frustration, difficulty, or crisis.

It's not a simple process. In basketball, rebounding involves an upward leap and aggressive grab, elbows out. You've got to protect the ball from others who may want it as much as you or more. After that, you must shoot, dribble, or pass the ball. And one rebound is not enough. If you rebound, then shoot and miss, you'll have to rebound again. (The "re" means again; "bound" means leap or jump.) Rebounding is what's required if at first you don't succeed. It's about leaping, again and again, defying gravity. It's how you "try, try, again."

What rebounding requires

So too with life. Sooner or later, it's going to involve mistakes, misfortunes, setbacks, frustrations, difficulties, crises. To rebound is to leap and grab a mistake, then transform it into something positive. Usually this is a repetitive process, and often it's exhausting. But it's essential.

Cathy Podvin developed rebounding skills while learning to in-line skate. It took her six months. "I can't tell you how many times I fell," she says. "I had to use my husband for support, or a hockey stick."

As Employee Relations Manager at Fifth Third Bank in Southfield, Michigan, Podvin now uses her rebounding skills on the job. "When you roll out a new program, you have high expectations, but sometimes you fall flat on your face," she admits. Last year, for instance, she created a Welcome Aboard program "that was supposed to be a nice, neat, orderly packet for all the managers to use to acclimate new employees into the organization. We worked it and worked it, trying to make it perfect, and based on early feedback, we thought it would hit the mark, but the managers thought it was too cumbersome, it was too much work, and they couldn't fit it into their daily schedule."

> Some days, you work so hard to help people, but you still fail. You feel horrible. But you still go back the next day.
>
> — Cathy Podvin

Bruised, Podvin had to pick herself up off the ground and try again. "It was difficult," she admits. "People had strong feelings about why it wasn't working. I had to lean on my manager. I had to re-check each individual step along the way."

When you fall off skates, Podvin says, it's scary. "I hate feeling out of control. And it hurts. I haven't broken any bones, but I've hurt myself."

Setbacks at the bank are difficult for similar reasons. "Disappointing. Out of control. Painful," says Podvin. "If my internal customers thank me for returning their calls, or appreciate my insight, or benefit from the way I help them with a staff problem, I feel like a champion. On days like that, you go home and feel great. On other days, you work so hard to help people, but you still fail. You lose the game. You go home and feel horrible.

"But you still go back the next day."

Podvin's story reminded me of Frances Willard's. The suffragist and President of the Women's Christian Temperance Union was 53 when she learned to ride the new form of transportation called the bicycle. She named hers Gladys (because it made her glad), and in 1895 she wrote a book about the experience called *A Wheel Within a Wheel: How I Learned to Ride the Bicycle.*

As with Podvin, learning the new skill took Willard six months, but she persisted despite "the sedentary habits of a lifetime," "the impedimenta that results from the unnatural style of dress," and the admonitions of loved ones who warned that she would break her bones. The parallels between sports and life became apparent to Willard, who explained, "That which caused the many failures I had in learning the bicycle had caused me failures in life; namely, a certain fearful looking for of judgement; a too vivid realization of the uncertainty of everything about me; an underlying doubt — at once, however (and this is all that saved me), matched and overcome by the determination not to give into it."[1]

Ultimately Willard concludes that "All failure was from a wobbling will rather than a wobbling wheel."[2]

Donna Lopiano pitched for the Raybestos Brakettes, the best women's softball team of all time, for nine years, leading them to six national championships, and has been inducted into the National Softball Hall of Fame. "The most important lesson I learned from sports was persistent effort and resilience: always giving your best effort and never giving up," says Lopiano. "Even when you lose a game, there's always another

> The rebounder risks getting pushed around, risks coming up empty-handed, risks shooting and missing again. He goes for it anyway.

game tomorrow and a chance to reassess, recommit, improve, and win." Executive director of the Women's Sports Foundation since 1992, Lopiano says that the foundation's primary mission — achieving gender equity in sports — requires that same persistence: "Educating the public with research-based facts, every day, every audience." Year after year, in a variety of ways, she reiterates her message: "The gift of sport is as important for our daughters as it is for our sons."

The rebounder keeps leaping for the ball, even when he's so embarrassed by his own poor shooting, or by the lopsided score, that he'd rather go shower. He risks getting pushed around, risks coming up empty-handed, risks shooting and missing again. He goes for it anyway.

Rebounding requires not only persistence and determination but also courage. The word courage comes from the French "coeur," for heart. The courageous person acts from the heart, pursuing her passion, even in the face of difficulty, disapproval from others, or disappointing results.

Courage is evident when you're afraid and you act from the heart anyway. If something doesn't scare you, it doesn't require courage. The difference between a courageous person and a coward is that the courageous person is not paralyzed by her fear.

Courage also enters the picture because we need to rebound not just from mistakes, but from misfortune. In the past few years, I've been touched by three close friends and family members who have rebounded from devastating grief after the sudden deaths of their children. One rebounded from her infant's death by mourning, creating a scholastic arts program in her daughter's memory, then having three more children. Another rebounded from her teen's death by creating a program to help other teens successfully navigate the perils of adolescence. The third rebounded from the death of her young-adult son by studying art and entering her paintings in exhibitions, thereby discovering a creative, meditative, and life-affirming practice. People rebound from misfortune in many other ways, too. The key is to find some reason to live so depression doesn't pin you to the ground.

Good rebounders: Job seekers who get rejected, then go for another interview. Politicians who lose, run again, lose, run again, lose, run again, win. Law students who fail the bar, fail the bar, fail the bar, pass. Two-year-olds who toddle, stumble, toddle, stumble, toddle, stumble, walk. Mourners who cry, talk, remember, let go, and embrace life.

Bad rebounders: Pouters. Pessimists. Risk-avoiders. People who can't admit their mistakes, or their aspirations. Insecure people, who don't believe they deserve to succeed. Out-of-shape people who tire easily and give up easily. Unimaginative people who don't know what to do with the ball once they catch it.

How to become a better rebounder: Practice rebounding. Expect great things of yourself, but also anticipate that some of your "shots" are not going to score. Be ready, just in case. Calculate how things might go wrong, and be prepared to respond in a constructive way. (See "G is for Goals.") Be patient, persistent, and self-forgiving. (See "F is for Forgiveness.") Interpret mistakes, misfortunes, setbacks, frustrations, and crises as missed shots in the game of life, unpredictable only in terms of "when," not "if."

Practice shooting (taking specific, focused steps to achieve your goals). Every time you miss, rebound and shoot again. After a while, you'll accept rebounding as part of the game. Rather than dwelling on missed shots, you'll proudly tally the number of times you have rebounded, the number of rebounds you have converted into points.

If you're going to become a good basketball player, you're going to miss a lot of shots. If you're going to become a successful dentist, technician, cashier, cab driver, babysitter, rancher, or executive, you're going to make mistakes. How you handle those mistakes will say a lot about who you are as a person, and will have a huge influence on your ultimate success.

In "Last Night as I was Sleeping," Antonio Machado describes a dream in which "golden bees" in his heart

> "were making white combs
> and sweet honey
> from my old failures."[3]

What a beautiful image. Within one's own heart, something delicious can be constructed out of "old failures." "Imagine the possibility," writes Roger Housden, commenting on this poem in his book, *Ten Poems to Change Your Life*, "that every single turn of events, however dark or disappointing the outcome, can in some circuitous way be the raw material for something that eventually surfaces with the sweetness of honey."

From this perspective, failures are not wrong. They're part of the process of life, as natural as getting up again when you fall down; as natural as a ball bouncing back into your hands.

R is for Rebound: Persist in the face of disappointment and defeat.

* * * * *

Time Out for Reflection

1) Describe a situation in which you tried, then tried again.

_____

_____

2) In what areas of your life are you good at persisting, rather than giving up?

_____

_____

3) What current situation challenges you to rebound repeatedly?

_____

_____

4) What could you do to become a better rebounder?

_____

_____

5) How are you going to motivate yourself to convert mistakes into something positive?

_____

_____

S is for Strong

Develop your physical power

S is for Strong
As in muscle and bone.
We need bodies to play with
Not mind games alone.

Weightlifter Cheryl Haworth recently set American records in the snatch (280.5 pounds) and the clean and jerk (341 pounds). She's not only strong, she's fast and flexible: she can run the 40-yard dash in 5.5 seconds, leap 30 inches, and do a split.

She's five-six, and weighs about 300 pounds. Like most weightlifters, she needs that body mass in order to lift huge amounts of weight overhead. It comes with the territory. The strongest people in the world are not skinny.

In the 2000 Olympics, the first time weightlifting was a women's sport, Haworth earned a bronze medal — an impressive accomplishment, especially since she was just seventeen. But instead of focusing on her achievement, reporters hounded her with absurd and offensive questions.

"What's it like to weigh so much?" they asked.

"Have you ever tried to lose weight?"

And, "How do the boys in your high school react to your weight?"

Finally, Haworth, a poised and focused young athlete, explained patiently: "I'm not trying to be small. I'm trying to be strong."

What a great answer! Haworth knows what she wants, and it's not having a flat tummy or wearing a size six dress. To her, success means being strong — specifically, the strongest woman in the world. Committed to that goal, her other decisions fall into place. (Haworth's reply is also a mission statement; see "P is for Purpose.")

Figuratively, many of us find it easier to be small (accommodating, fitting in, taking up little space) than to be strong (assertive, authoritative, influential.) Strong people risk social censure, failure, and the loneliness of the limelight.

But let's get literal. Physical health and strength provide a foundation for success, whether you're short or tall, petite or grand. Health and strength are not absolutely necessary — think of Stephen Hawking, Christopher Reeve — but a strong body can certainly facilitate the development of a strong mind, and a successful career.

Better than any drug: Daily physical exercise

How can one build and sustain strength? There is only one answer: Daily physical exercise. Is that bad news? It can sound dreary, but once you lace up your sneakers and walk out the door, it can become downright exhilarating, some days. Other days it's just something you do because you're committed to your physical and mental health. Because you're an athlete, and that's what athletes do. On those days you don't much enjoy the process, but you feel great afterward, when you take a deep breath and the breath seems to fill your whole body, down to your toes. Or you lean over to lift a 40-pound bag of dog food and realize you can do it much more easily than before. Or you travel, getting in and out of cramped spaces, and arrive at your destination feeling fine. Or you walk, just a simple distance from one room to another, and notice that your leg muscles feel solid and strong. Next thing you know, you're grinning.

> I'm not trying to be small.
> I'm trying to be strong.
> — weightlifter Cheryl Haworth

Until recently, George Heavey was in charge of 12,000 customs officers, managing 300 points of entry along the perimeter of United States. "Our job is the detection and interdiction of contraband, including illegal drugs — and terrorists," explained Heavey shortly before he retired as Executive Director of the Office of Field Operations for the US Customs Service. "We're the front line in the nation's defense of its border."

As one might imagine, Heavey's work environment since September 11, 2001 has included "enormous levels of stress, intensity, law enforcement events, movement of customs inspectors to the northern border, collaboration with the National Guard and immigration services, terrorist threats day in and day out, and lots of decisions to be made — by me," says Heavey.

Fortunately, Heavey swims. "When I walk into the office after swimming for an hour, I am at peace with myself," he says. "I am in control of my emotions and clear-headed. Everyone else is all jazzed up, and I'm Mr. Stability, Mr. Laid Back, Mr. Mellow. The classic thing to say is that you learn from sports how to compete in the workplace, but I don't need to be any more competitive in the workplace. Swimming helps me find my sense of balance and equilibrium. After my morning swim, I'm at peace — and when you're dealing with a war-room environment, that's a big help."

Only about thirty percent of adults exercise several times a week, according to a 2002 National Health Interview Survey. Almost forty percent of adults are sedentary, essentially never exercising.

Daily physical exercise can take innumerable forms depending on your personality, age, interests, and abilities: aerobics, aikido, archery, badminton, baseball, basketball, bodybuilding, bowling, canoeing, crew, cycling, darts, diving, dogsledding, equestrian events, fencing, field hockey, figure skating, golf, gymnastics, handball, hang-gliding, heptathlon, ice hockey, judo, jumping rope, karate, kayaking, lacrosse, marathoning, mountain climbing, New Games, obstacle courses, orienteering, pentathlon, Ping-Pong, quidditch, running, sailing, skiing, scuba diving, snorkeling, snowboarding, soccer, softball, surfing, swimming, T'ai Chi, tennis, track and field, triathlon, ultimate Frisbee, underwater hockey, volleyball, walking, water polo, weightlifting, wheelchair sports, windsurfing, X-games, yachting, yoga, and, well, I can't think of a sport that starts with a Z. (Can you?) But you get my point, I hope. There's a world of activity out there, and if we're going to think of ourselves as athletes, at some point we're going to need to move. At some point, thinking will not be sufficient. We will feel an urgent desire to act the way athletes act, not only off the playing fields, but also on them.

The best exercise for you? The one you're willing to do.

Many studies have shown that regular, moderate exercise can:

1) Lower the heart rate by strengthening the heart muscle
2) Reduce the risk of heart disease and heart failure
3) Reduce the risk of stroke
4) Reduce the risk of breast cancer
5) Decrease blood pressure
6) Slow the progression of osteoporosis by strengthening bones
7) Offset the pain and inconvenience of arthritis
8) Lower low-density lipoproteins (LDL), aiding in controlling cholesterol
9) Decrease the chance of developing Type II diabetes
10) Increase pain tolerance
11) Reduce the risk of colon cancer
12) Elevate mood, reducing depression and anxiety
13) Strengthen and maintain healthy muscles
14) Prevent back and other injuries
15) Improve weight loss and maintenance
16) Increase mental capacity
17) Improve metabolism and digestion
18) Improve sleep
19) Improve sexual function

20) Increase energy

21) Lessen the severity and frequency of pain from clogged arteries in the legs

"If exercise could be packed into a pill," says Robert N. Butler, M.D., Director of the National Institute on Aging, "it would be the single most widely prescribed, and beneficial, medicine in the nation."

Physical conditioning becomes increasingly important with age. "Typically, beginning in middle age, aerobic capacity and muscle mass go down about ten percent per decade," says Jerome Fleg, a researcher studying the health benefits of exercise at the National Heart, Lung, and Blood Institute. At about age sixty, physical decline accelerates. But most of the physical changes attributed to getting old — including decreased lung function, decreased muscle mass, high blood pressure, and insulin resistance — are not due to aging, but to a sedentary lifestyle, new research verifies. A 2002 *New England Journal of Medicine* study of more than 6,000 older men showed that poor physical fitness was a better predictor of premature death than smoking, hypertension, or heart disease. Several recent studies of seniors aged 60 to 90+ have shown that regular aerobic and weight-lifting sessions improve muscle mass by 50 to 80 percent, enabling some to discard canes and walkers, walk faster, and climb stairs more easily.

Exercise helps keep weight down — increasingly important in our increasingly overweight society. A 2002 study by the AARP (formerly the American Association of Retired Persons) finds that among 50- to 64-year-olds, more than a quarter (26.7 percent) are not just overweight but clinically obese, up from 14.4 percent in 1982. Obesity — which is also on the rise in people over 64 — increases the risk of diabetes, high blood pressure, and heart disease.[1]

> There is no drug in current or prospective use that holds as much promise for a life of extended vitality as does physical exercise.
>
> — Walter Michael Bortz II, Stanford University professor

"There is no drug in current or prospective use that holds as much promise for a life of extended vitality as does physical exercise," says Walter Michael Bortz II, a professor of medicine at Stanford University. "Fitness becomes a survival issue."[2]

Flexibility

Just as power must always be closely associated with rest (see "E is for Endurance"), so, too, strength has a twin, a quality without which strength becomes meaningless. Strength's twin is flexibility.

As Cheryl Haworth demonstrates with her splits, even the strongest people in the world need to be flexible. For muscles (as well as minds) to receive nourishment and function well over time, they must stretch. This is why health clubs offer not only weights and weight machines but yoga classes, stretching rooms, and massages.

At my age (middle), I stretch twice a day. That may sound extreme, but as an active athlete (an hour a day of swimming or weightlifting, plus weekend golf), I need it. Three days a week, I stretch for about five minutes in the morning, then again for five minutes at night, each time adding another five minutes of "core stability" exercises to keep my lower back and torso strong. (All strength originates in the center of the body, so bulging biceps will do you no good if your back and abdominal muscles are weak.) Three days a week, I extend the morning stretch to fifteen or twenty minutes, incorporating yoga in addition to the core stability work. One day a week, I do an hour of yoga. In this way, I keep my muscles supple, ready to do their work (walking, sitting, standing, speaking, weight-lifting, suitcase-lifting, travelling, swimming, golfing) and also ready to relax when I need them to, like at night. It's a "D" thing ("D" is for Discipline.)

I can't say what your muscles need. You probably can, if you listen. The more one thinks of oneself as an athlete, the more one begins to tune in to the language of the body, the various ways it talks to the brain about what's going on, what it needs, and how that changes over time. (See "K is for Knowledge.")

How to begin (or begin again) an exercise program

"I've been out of shape for so long, I don't remember how to get back in shape," people tell me, despairing. Do not despair. Lots of people get in shape, even late in life. To begin an exercise program, set one very small, very achievable goal, such as walking for ten minutes from 7:00 to 7:10 on Monday mornings or evenings. That's all. Finding an extra ten minutes in a week can be a challenge, and changing habits can be difficult, so the key is to take a tiny step in the right direction. Do that one small thing for a month or two, keeping a log of your accomplishments. Even making a check mark on a calendar can give you a visual confirmation that you're on the right track. Once you've accomplished that small goal, expand it: maybe ten minutes of walking two or three times a week. Then do that for a month or two.

The key is to choose something very "doable" so you don't get discouraged and don't give up. Even so, you will hear voices (we all do) that say you don't have time, you don't have the right clothing, you don't like exercise, it won't do any good, etc. Don't take these voices seriously, but don't expect them to go away, either. Tell them, "Thank you very much for your opinion," then proceed. Do not let them prevail. You know better. Soon the physical and mental benefits of taking care of your body will provide their own incentive, and their own momentum.

Your physical health matters. Strength and flexibility are essential and interesting psychological qualities, too: we need to be assertive and receptive, determined and open-minded. But let's not go there today, not in this chapter. When I say that in order to spell success you need to be both strong and supple, I mean that literally. I'm directing your attention to your body, gently reminding you to devote some time each day to physical exercise.

S is for Strong: Develop your physical power.

* * * * *

Time Out for Reflection

1) Was there a time in your life when you were stronger and more physically fit than you are now? Compare how you felt then and now.

_____

_____

2) How do you (or could you) develop and maintain physical strength on a daily basis?

_____

_____

3) Regardless of how physically fit you are already, what small step could you take to further your commitment to personal, physical strength and flexibility?

_____

_____

T is for Teamwork

Seek and support people who are on your side

T is for Teamwork
Who's on your side?
Whom do you trust?
Who's along for your ride?

After September 11, 2001, sports took a bad rap. People called them "trivial," "simply diversions," and "just entertainment." Journalists pledged never again to refer to athletes as heroic. Among the true heroes, everyone now agreed, were the passengers and flight attendants on United Flight 93, who apparently sabotaged the hijackers' plan and saved the lives of people on the ground. Athletes, by contrast, merely play games.

I see it differently. In the process of playing games, athletes develop courage, confidence, and commitment. They might never need to demonstrate "true" heroism of the hijacked-plane variety. But through discipline, goal-setting, competition, teamwork, and leadership, they develop skills that can help them in numerous other endeavors, from professional pursuits to parenting.

In fact, the passengers on Flight 93 included a former collegiate judo champion, a retired paratrooper, a weightlifter, a flight attendant who was a former police officer, a lawyer with a brown belt in karate, a former collegiate rugby player, and a former football quarterback.[1] Did athletic training help these people summon the confidence to think clearly under pressure, work as a team, take a risk? It seems so.

Having learned via cell phones that three jets had already crashed into the Pentagon and the World Trade Center's twin towers, the passengers and crew asked family members and supervisors for advice and prayers, then calmly planned a revolt.

Passenger Thomas Burnett, a former high school quarterback, told his wife, Deena, that he and two other passengers were talking about "rushing the hijackers."

Passenger Mark Bingham, a six-five former University of California, Berkeley rugby player, did not mention the plan to his mother, Alice Hoglan, whom he called, but she speculates that he joined the other passengers in the fight. Mark was "a team player who knew how to motivate and inspire people," she told *Sports Illustrated*. He was also courageous, having once grabbed a gun from the hands of a would-be assailant. After listening to the cockpit recording, Hoglan said, "We heard enough to convince us that there were some true heroes on board, and the terrorists were frightened. There was an amazing assemblage of take-charge, resourceful people used to acting decisively and as a team, and we heard them urging each other on."[2]

Passenger Todd Beamer, using a phone on the plane, reached a GTE supervisor and told her about the hijacking; she told him what had happened in New York and the Pentagon. Beamer asked her to pray with him, asked her to call his wife, and explained that he and others were going to jump on a hijacker who claimed to be wearing a bomb. Before he dropped the phone, the supervisor heard these legendary words, addressed to his ad-hoc teammates: "Let's roll."

Passenger Jeremy Glick, a ski instructor, rugby player, and former national judo champion, conferred with his wife, Lyz, a former gymnast and diver who coaches gymnastics at a New Jersey high school. The plane was already circling back toward Washington, D.C., just a half hour from the city. He and others were debating whether to rush the hijackers, he told her, and they were taking a vote.

"He was asking me, 'I need some advice — we're talking about attacking these men. What should I do?' I was scared about giving him the wrong information. I didn't want to do something wrong and have something terrible happen, and so I asked him if they were armed. And he said he had seen knives. But there were no guns.

"I finally just decided: 'Honey, you need to go for it.'

"We said 'I love you' a thousand times over and over again, and it just brought so much peace to us," says Lyz. "He told me, 'I love Emmy' — who is our daughter — and to take care of her. Then he said, 'Whatever decisions you make in your life, I need you to be happy, and I will respect any decisions that you make.' That gives me the most comfort. He sounded strong.

"Neither of us panicked. He knew that he was not going to make it out of there."

The crew also played a role. Sandra Bradshaw, 38, a flight attendant from Greensboro, North Carolina, phoned her husband, Philip, a US Airways pilot who was at home, and asked him for prayers and suggestions. She then told him that the flight attendants were boiling water to throw on the hijackers. Her last words: "We're all running to first class. I've got to go. Bye."

Apparently these brave people (and perhaps others), buoyed by their contacts with the outside world, then stormed the cockpit. Soon afterward, the plane crashed in the Pennsylvania countryside, killing all 44 people on board. Investigators now believe that the uprising thwarted the hijackers' plan to dive-bomb the plane into the White House.

Glick's family members believe his athletic training was instrumental in enabling him to take heroic action. "Sports allowed Jeremy to think under pressure," says his younger sister, Joanna, an ice skater and cross country runner. "And sports always teaches you there is no separation into groups. You come together, you work as one."[3]

Jeremy's sister Jennifer was a hurdler in high school and played field hockey in college; Jeremy's three brothers all wrestled. "Sports has been such a wonderful influence in our children's lives," says their mother, Joan. (In his honor, Glick's family created a foundation called Jeremy's Heroes to help young people develop character through sport.[4])

Other examples of September 11 teamwork abound. Recall the rescue workers searching the mountain of rubble that used to be the World Trade Center. Steel beams on their shoulders and hard hats on their heads, these ironworkers, carpenters, electricians, heavy equipment operators, and other volunteers coordinated their efforts to haul away debris and uncover survivors. Meanwhile, at the Pentagon, crews worked eighteen hours a day to repair the damaged building, inspired by a neon sign: "Let's roll." Remember the firefighters and military personnel who hung a giant flag next to the gaping hole at the Pentagon? Their effort provided the nation with a powerful symbol of unity, pride, hope, and strength. The team spirit spread throughout the United States and to other nations as millions of people offered time, expertise, and money to help the survivors and the victims' families.

> **One finger can't lift a pebble.**
>
> — Hopi saying

Most of us, thank goodness, are never called upon to save lives. But we do have opportunities to work with others to achieve mutual goals, and the more we know about teamwork, the better we can achieve those goals.

Good to great

After examining 1435 companies and evaluating the 11 that went from "good to great," mountain climber and business executive Jim Collins concluded that a leader's vision isn't as important as teamwork. "Most people assume that great bus drivers (read: business leaders) immediately start the journey by announcing to the people on the bus where they're going — by setting a new direction or by articulating a fresh corporate vision," says Collins.[5]

"In fact, leaders of companies that go from good to great start not with "where" but with "who." They start by getting the right people on the bus, the wrong people off the bus, and the right people in the right seats."

Joseph Campbell defines heroes as people who "test themselves, put themselves in unfamiliar territory, risk their identity, and come back from an ordeal or an adventure with a gift for the community." But Campbell is citing ancient myths that tend to see the hero as an individual actor. Team sport athletes see it differently. We take risks, but we don't have to take them alone. We test ourselves, but not apart from the community. Rather, we work together with other community members to create a stronger team.

In fact, in most endeavors, teamwork is not optional. As the Hopi say, "One finger can't lift a pebble."

The six qualities of solid teams

Here are the six qualities teams need most:

1) Teams need shared goals.

There's a difference between friends and teammates. Friends are people who like you. Teammates are people who support you to achieve your goals. Teammates may or may not like you. But they want you to succeed.

A friend might say, "I don't want to work on this project with you because it might hurt our relationship." A teammate would say, "Of course I'll do it with you. We share the same vision and passion, so we'll be successful."

For a teammate to support you to achieve your individual goals, you have to tell him or her what your goals are. In order to do that, you have to clarify exactly what they are in quantifiable terms. And for a team to achieve goals together, those goals must be articulated so everyone understands them and agrees to work toward them.

2) Teams need a sense of "we."

Before they come to believe "we can," teams need to know who "we" are. They need a team identity (uniforms, jargon, and secret handshakes help), along with team values.

On an athletic team, it's easy to identify your teammates: they wear the same uniform as you. Off the playing fields, it can be more difficult to decide who's included in that "we." Everyone in the company? Everyone in the family? Everyone in your religious, political, or social organization? Everyone in your country?

Who are your teammates? Who would help you in a crisis? Who volunteers — or would volunteer, if you'd ask — to help you shoulder your ordinary responsibilities?

Look around you and decide who supports you to achieve your goals, or would, if they knew what your goals were. These people may change from day to day or year to year, but it's a good idea to figure out who they are. Your answers may surprise you.

The "we" must also include the people "on the bench" — the "second stringers" who inevitably feel they're not contributing as much as they could. These are the people on the team — in the company or family or organization — who believe they're not getting the recognition they deserve. They need extra attention, appreciation, and chances to play the game. From their vantage point on the bench, they see things others do not see. They need to be included and listened to.

3) Teams need affection and appreciation.

"The playing of a game has to do with your feelings, your emotions, how you care about the people you're involved with," says Rutgers women's basketball coach Vivian Stringer.

You don't have to approve of your teammates' beliefs, their lifestyle, the way they chew gum. You do have to care about them as people, and respect them as unique individuals who have strengths and weaknesses, just as you do. You need to express genuine appreciation and even affection for them, even when these people are very different from you. In this process, you develop valuable relationship skills.

"Sports aren't about awards or world championships, though those are great," says soccer champion Mia Hamm. "They're about the relationships we have with one another."

When I speak to business groups, the complaint I hear most often from women is, "The women in my office don't support each other." Girls who don't have athletic experience — and who learn to compete only over beauty and boyfriends — often grow up to be women who don't bond in the workplace, don't share information, don't mentor. These women tend to wait for other people to be good "team players," and complain when others don't do this, rather than taking the initiative themselves.

"A sense of teamwork begins with individual action," I explain to them, asking, "When's the last time you complimented a colleague on her success?"

I swim on a masters team, training with a small group of women and men who swim at about my speed. Some of us have been doing this together, sharing Lane Three, for more than ten years. We know each other's speeds and rhythms and bodies; we can tell when someone has a sore shoulder; we notice (but politely refrain from commenting upon) each other's post-Thanksgiving bulges. We're very compatible, very supportive. And

> The playing of a game has to do with your feelings, your emotions, how you care about the people you're involved with.
>
> — Rutgers women's basketball coach Vivian Stringer

here's what I notice: When I say to Cynthia, for example, "Gee, you look really fast today," she gets faster. Same thing happens when Sue compliments me on my speed. I speed up, or sustain that same speed in a way that I might not have if Sue hadn't commented on it. It's nice to be noticed, to have an audience of any size. Such support leads not only to good feelings among the teammates, but to faster times.

So too in the workplace, and in the home. When we offer each other compliments, these compliments affect behavior as well as mood. If you want to increase productivity among your teammates, try letting them know you admire what they're doing. Then sit back and watch.

4) Teams need trust.

When my Stanford basketball team was losing, my teammates trusted me to score. So they would pass me the ball, then expect me to shoot, and I would, trusting that the ball would go in.

Sometimes the ball went in, sometimes it didn't. But their trust in me, along with my trust in myself, made it more likely that I would succeed.

Their trust was not unfounded. It was based on my skill. But their trust also enhanced my skill. It was a gift that helped me to excel. If they had not trusted me, I might have worried, "What if I miss?" Because they trusted me, I expected success. When you expect success, you're more likely to achieve it.

Chamique Holdsclaw names trust as the most important attribute in a teammate. "A teammate is someone who has your back," says Holdsclaw, captain of the Washington Mystics. "You develop this over time, on and off the court. You talk, you listen, you see who you can trust. Then this gets played out on the floor. Can I trust her to play her position? If I get beat, can I trust her to pick up the slack?"

5) Teams need to communicate.

On a basketball court, the players on defense are always talking to each other. You might not hear it from the stands, but they're saying, "Cutter through the lane," "Watch #24," "I've got her," "Shot," etc.

What they mean is: "Here's some information I have that will help us reach our goals." "Here's my suggestion for how you can do your job better." "Just a reminder: I'm helping you; you have my full support." "Let's pay attention together, and together we will succeed."

6) Teams need leadership.

Every team needs a leader or leaders. These people may have a designated leadership title or not, may be quiet or boisterous, serious or funny. But they must lead by example and also encourage others to perform their best.

C. Lynn Centonze, Chief of Police in Fairfield, New Jersey, says her leadership style is to empower her line officers. "I trust them so thoroughly. I need to. They can go into a domestic violence call and make good decisions about who should be arrested, how the whole thing should be handled. If I paralyzed them by second guessing them, it could cost them their lives. For their safety and the safety of the public, I need to trust them, and that means all of them."

If you want to experience the joys and successes of teamwork, be a good teammate yourself. Offer assistance and support, especially when you're "on the bench": not being the star. Reaching out to praise or assist someone else can feel good to both of you. Request help when you need it, too; many people appreciate being asked for their opinion or advice. And celebrate often. Successful working teams — like successful sports teams and successful search-and-rescue teams — celebrate even small successes to keep morale high.

Life is a team sport. Everyone needs people to play with: editors, supervisors, managers, bosses, colleagues, partners, spouses. Seek people who will bring out the best in you: the best performance, the best character, the best opportunities to learn and grow — and take responsibility for bringing out the best in others, too.

Teammates might be people you've known all your life, or people you just met on an airplane. You share a goal and a commitment to reach that goal. With that common vision, all things become possible.

T is for Teamwork: Seek and support people who are on your side.

*   *   *   *   *

TIME OUT FOR REFLECTION

1) Who are your true teammates in your personal life? Name two.

_____

_____

2) Who are your teammates in school or at work? Name two.

_____

_____

3) What sort of relationship do you want to have with your teammates? Who is in charge of that?

_____

_____

4) Do your teammates know your goals?

_____

_____

5) Describe a time when you successfully cooperated with other people. How did you feel about yourself and the experience?

_____

_____

6) What is one specific thing you can do to strengthen your sense of team and team spirit?

_____

_____

U is for Uniqueness

Take pride in your stride

U is for Uniqueness
Do your own thing.
Play your own game.
Find your own swing.

Everywhere I go, people ask, "How tall are you, anyway?"

Most of the time, I don't think about being tall. I can walk to the bank, deposit a check, return home, and never once think about being tall. When I rent a video, it's not "Get Shorty." When I screw in a light bulb without standing on a chair, I am not amazed.

But apparently this is a burning question for people. They actually chase me down the street, shouting, "How tall are you, anyway?"

Ann Landers says I don't have to answer this question any more than fat people have to answer how much they weigh. But I don't mind. So I say, "Six-two."

> **Have you always been that tall?**

They inevitably respond, "You don't *look* that tall."

Well then: Why are you chasing me down the street?

People also tell me, as if this might be news to me: "You're tall!" And they confess: "I wish I were tall." Then they add: "But not as tall as you."

They also ask a series of questions, all of which are difficult to answer:

"What's it like being so tall?"

"How did you get to be so tall?"

"Have you always been that tall?"

Permission to be outstanding

It was my mother who gave me permission to stand up straight, to stand out, to be outstanding, to be my whole unique self. Mom's five-ten and a half. She never leaves off that half inch. She's proud of being tall, as if it were a personal accomplishment. Dad's six-three, my brother's six-four, and my sister's only five-nine, but she always wears heels so she doesn't feel too short around the rest of us.

We didn't have a strong ethnic or national identity — we're English, French, Irish, Scottish, Dutch, German, Norwegian, and Swedish — and Mom wanted us to have *some* identity, so she decided we should be the Tall Family. She taught us to have Tall Pride, to do Tall Bonding, and to say, "Tall is beautiful."

She would measure us every three weeks or so, lining us up against a cloth wallhanging of Jack and his beanstalk. The goal was to grow as tall as highest bean. Mom would mark our heights with pencil, date them, then consult her Metropolitan Life charts. I was always off the charts. Apparently they didn't make other children that tall. I remember Mom proudly announcing: "Mariah, you are now three inches taller than the average six-year-old!" She thought this was terrific.

Mom also taught us to identify with other tall people. She would point out tall people wherever we went, as if we couldn't see for ourselves who was tall. "There's a tall woman," she would say. But because Mom's competitive, she would add, "But you have better posture."

Recently, while vacationing with Mom over the holidays, we saw the University of Kansas women's basketball team in the lobby of our hotel. "Go stand next to them," she urged me. "I want to see who's taller."

Mom also enjoys networking. She'll say, "There's a tall woman, Mariah. Go ask her where she buys big shoes."

A while ago, I realized that all this time, Mom hasn't been talking about height. She has been giving me permission to be outstanding. To be myself. And to be head and shoulders, literally or figuratively, above the rest.

For a tall child, simply standing up can mean standing out, and standing out can feel risky. And for a tall girl, in a society that still tells girls they should be dainty, delicate, decorative, and deferential, it takes courage to be outstanding. Mom helped me develop that courage.

Athletes can't be shy

Sports helped too. Athletes can't be shy. They can't worry about intimidating other people with their height, their strength, their skill. In fact, in sports it's good to stand out, to be outstanding, to be different.

Paradoxically, by challenging us to play certain games within certain rules, sports enable us to be truly, authentically ourselves. Bodies are as individual as faces, so when people run or swim or ski, no two of them move through space or water or snow the same way. Even team sport athletes bring to the playing fields unique ways of accomplishing physical goals, as well as unique ways of interacting with other players.

A basketball coach can show you where to put your fingers, your palm, your elbow. She can demonstrate: This is how to shoot a free throw. But you'll never release a ball the exact same way she does, and you

> We all have a physical, psychological, and even spiritual need to express our creativity.

shouldn't. Your height, weight, muscle mass, bone density, strength, flexibility, energy level, metabolism, coordination, desire, vision, hearing, proprioception, and ability to focus will come into play, as well as your internal experience of motion and joy: what feels good to you. This is why no two gymnasts doing the exact same routine to the exact same music look the same to the audience, or trigger the same emotional experience in them.

Until you understand this, you can waste a lot of time trying to swing a golf club like Karrie Webb. Imitate her swing to your heart's content, but ultimately it's your body you've got to work with, not hers, so you'll have to find your own swing, and therein lies a lifetime quest, not only for golfers, but for all of us.

We worry about the influence of peer pressure on teenagers but we'd all be wise to become aware of the peer pressure adults experience, and transcend it. How many of us feel "completely ourselves" at a party, at a business meeting, in the grocery store? How often do we try to hide our unique expressions of love or pleasure or sadness in order to fit in? Don't all of us cover our true feelings and desires with conventional behaviors, speech patterns, and even dress?

Our leadership styles, our teaching styles, our negotiation styles, our communication styles — all have been influenced by others we've observed. Same for our choice of jobs, homes, cities or towns. But to be most effective, we have to find our own swings, so to speak: our own ways of accomplishing goals. All of us are unique. We all have a physical, psychological, and even spiritual need to express our creativity.

I'm thankful to Mom for encouraging me to stand up straight. I'm glad to have good posture. It communicates confidence to others, and helps me feel good about myself. But beyond the physical training in How to Be Tall, Mom taught me a deeper lesson about finding — over and over again — the courage to be outstanding, to be my own authentic self. In my case, this has helped me create a unique career, first as an athlete, then as an author and speaker.

We all have unique bodies, abilities and gifts. Understand and embrace exactly who you are, and your uniqueness will lead the way toward professional and personal success.

U is for Uniqueness: Take pride in your stride.

* * * * *

TIME OUT FOR REFLECTION

1) What is one way in which you are different from many other people?

_____

_____

2) Do you take pride in that difference, or it is a source of discomfort or embarrassment? Explain.

_____

_____

3) When is a time when you were outstanding? How did it feel to stand out?

_____

_____

4) What is one unique aspect of yourself that you'd like to cultivate, at work or at home?

_____

_____

5) How might you change if you allowed yourself to be all of who you are?

_____

_____

V is for Voice

Speak up and speak out for what's right

V is for Voice
Speak up. Claim your share.
Athletes succeed when
They openly care.

Some of us settle for less than we're worth, less than we could achieve, less than we could hope for if we dared to assert our needs, claim our space, insist on full and equal opportunity. Many of us — especially women, people of color, gay people, disabled people, immigrants — get accustomed to being second class citizens. It comes to feel natural to us; it's the water we swim in. So we don't speak up.

I saw this dynamic at work when I served as the assistant varsity girls' coach for a metropolitan Washington, D.C. high school in the mid-nineties. When I arrived at the school, there were three other girls' coaches, all women in their twenties. "We have two gyms," they told me. "One for the girls, one for the boys."

"Uh-oh," I said. "Are they the same size?"

"Oh no," they explained, showing me around. The teeny tiny one, so small there was no room for bleachers, was the girls' gym. The larger one — which seated about 1500 — was for the boys.

"Uh-oh," I said again. I was having déjà vu all over again, as Yogi Berra might have said. I had lived through this before, more than twenty years ago.

My first two years at Stanford, we played in Roble Gym — which was so claustrophobic that our twenty or so fans sat on a single bench between the sideline and the wall. Our basketball coach was a kind, devoted, unpaid graduate student. We bought our own high-tops and taped our own ankles. For uniforms, we wore red shorts and white t-shirts, over which we tied red "pinnies."

> We were angry. We were persistent. We were, I'm sure, a pain in the neck.

I have come to think of us as the "pinney generation."

We were miserable. Two of my teammates (Sonia Jarvis and Stephanie Erickess-Caluya) and I spent all our free time in athletic director Dick DiBiaso's office, demanding equal treatment with the men. We'd drop by unannounced, insist on meeting with Mr. DiBiaso, then remind him that Title IX, the federal law that prohibits discrimination on the basis of sex in educational institutions, had passed two years earlier, in 1972. It was his job to implement it, we informed him.

We were angry. We were persistent. We were, I'm sure, a pain in the neck.

Finally, in my junior year, we moved into Maples Pavilion, which seats 7,400 fans. (That's not big by today's standards, but Stanford men and women still play there.) We received uniforms, a trainer, and access to the weight room. Stanford hired our first two coaches: Dotty McCrea, who had been an assistant to Cathy Rush at three-time national champion Immaculata College, and Sue Rojcewicz, who came to Stanford directly from the 1976 Olympics, where she had helped the United States win a silver medal.

My senior year, Stanford granted its first basketball scholarship. The next year, all twelve players were on scholarship. In 1990, Stanford won its first national championship. They did it again in 1992, and they've been one of the nation's top programs ever since, winning the Sears Cup, awarded to the nation's best college for women's and men's sports, for five years in a row.

My teammates and I don't take credit for Stanford's success. But I do think our voices mattered, as do all voices that speak up on behalf of what's right.

Ironically, speaking up for myself and my team was a lesson that I had already learned on the basketball court. Players demand, "Give me the ball!" They yell, "Help!" They say, "That was out of bounds." They get in the habit of asserting their rights to score, to succeed, to play fair.

A tale of two gyms

So of course I spoke up again when I started coaching the high school girls' team in the Washington, D.C. area. "This is not right," I said to the other girls' coaches. "Why should the boys play in the big gym, while the girls play in the small gym? Title IX outlawed such blatant discrimination more than twenty years ago." I proposed that the varsity girls and boys share the big gym, and the younger girls and boys share the small gym.

What amazed me was this: None of the other girls' coaches wanted to go along with my plan. All three of them were women — young women. But they had grown comfortable with the small gym. They called it the girls' gym.

"This is the way it's always been," they said. "Ever since they built the boys' gym for the boys."

"What sort of statement are we making to our girls?" I asked them.

"Our offices are here," they protested, "near the girls' gym. If we played in the boys' gym, we'd have to carry the basketballs all the way down the hall."

"Since when is basketball transportation a major hardship on a coach?" I asked. "And besides, why are your offices near the small gym, while the men's offices are near the big gym?"

> Individual voices, sometimes joined into a chorus, have served as a catalyst for change throughout our history.

Eventually I persuaded the girls' coaches to support my proposal. Together we approached the athletic director — who was a woman. She readily agreed that we were right. But she had worked at the school for several years, and had not spoken up. She, too, had grown comfortable with "the girls' gym."

Finally we asked the boys' head coach if the girls and boys could share the big gym equally. He said okay. He had been at the school ever since Title IX had passed, so he'd been expecting this for more than 20 years. He didn't fight against us. But nor had he fought *for* us. All those years, and he hadn't seen it as his responsibility to give the girls equal access to the big gym. Like many other people in positions of authority, he had not spoken up for the victims of discrimination.

Our girls were delighted. So were their parents. The boys, however, were resentful. It was Laurie Priest, Mount Holyoke's athletic director, who pointed out to me that when girls or women are given equal opportunities, boys and men often feel discriminated against. They're so used to having privilege, they sometimes feel like 50/50 is unfair.

At the same time, men (politicians, lawyers, scholars, authors, activists) play a vital role in the women's movement, and have for more than a century, ever since the goal was suffrage. Fathers and male coaches now speak up on behalf of the rights of female athletes, insisting that softball fields be comparable to baseball fields, for instance, or complaining to the school board when the girls' crew team uses older equipment than the boys' team.

Individual voices, sometimes joined into a chorus, have served as a catalyst for change throughout our history. Recall how Rosa Parks "spoke up" by refusing to relinquish her seat on the bus to a white man, and how Martin Luther King eloquently voiced his vision in his "I have a dream" speech. Nowadays women's voices are shattering the glass ceiling at work; when female employees speak up, speak out, and assert their opinions and needs, things change. Often at great personal risk, "whistleblowers" are holding corporations and government agencies accountable for their practices. Male college athletes are speaking up, refusing to endure insulting and offensive coaching practices. And because brave young men and women are coming forward and telling their stories, the Catholic Church is being held accountable for its history of sexual abuse and cover-ups.

But as you can see from my experiences with the passive coaches and athletic director, many of us fear rocking the boat, making waves, drowning in a sea of resentment and resistance. Even if we learned from sports how to speak up, we don't necessarily do it on the job, or in our communities. When we're in the minority, we often speak in quiet, accommodating voices, trying to avoid attention or criticism. It can be scary to speak up, on behalf or ourselves or others. But that's the only way things change.

V is for Voice: Speak up and speak out for what's right.

* * * * *

Time Out for Reflection

1) How do you decide when to speak up and when not to?

_____

_____

2) When was a specific time you benefited by raising problems, concerns, suggestions? Describe what happened.

_____

_____

3) Are you involved in a situation that is unfair? If so, what, if anything, is keeping you from voicing your opinion about it? Who has the power to change things?

_____

_____

W is for Winning

Give yourself permission to be the best

W is for Winning
And losing, its brother
To love one twin sibling
You must love the other.

Several years ago, while coaching a local high school basketball team, I noticed something odd about our best player, a six-foot sophomore guard named Michelle. During games, she was agile and confident. Yet before games, when her name was announced, she would shuffle onto the court, head down and shoulders hunched.

Finally I asked her, "Michelle, why do you walk like that? Aren't you proud of yourself?"

Michelle replied, "I'm embarrassed to be the best."

Oh dear, I thought. This was 1994, not 1954. I wanted to lecture her. "Have you no idea how many women over the years have worked hard to get you to this position where you can develop your talent, where you can play each week in front of hundreds of adoring parents and peers, where you can work toward a full athletic scholarship to a major university? Embarrassed to be the best? Michelle, it's good to be the best! Hasn't anyone told you that yet?"

Fortunately I managed to skip the lecture. Instead I asked, "Who do you look up to?" — hoping she'd say, "You, Mariah."

"Sheryl Swoopes," she said. Swoopes had scored 47 points for Texas Tech to lead them to the NCAA championship title two seasons before that.

"How does Sheryl carry herself?" I asked. Michelle lifted her head, inflated her chest, and immediately began to look like Sheryl Swoopes. "Would you like to win a national championship with your college basketball team someday?" I asked.

"Yes," Michelle said timidly.

"Then you're going to have to act like Sheryl," I informed her. "You already have her disciplined work ethic, her competitive spirit, her willingness to learn and be coached. You just need to start giving yourself permission to be the best, as Sheryl does. You need to be willing to win, even among your teammates."

From that day on, Michelle walked onto the court pretending she was Sheryl Swoopes. As the season progressed, her posture changed and her role on the team changed. She began acting like a leader. She also made progress toward her goal, developing an A Game that had previously eluded her. Two years later, Michelle entered Purdue University on full athletic scholarship. Two years after that, she was in the starting lineup as Purdue won the national championship — not because she had a terrific high school basketball coach (though she did!) — but because she gave herself permission to win.

> I came out here to beat everybody in sight and that's just what I'm going to do.
>
> — Babe Didrikson

This might seem like a girl thing. The best player on the boys' team at Michelle's high school was not embarrassed by his own excellence. He was more than willing to stand out. It's girls and women who worry what others will think of us. We want *everyone* to be the best — and in an attempt to achieve that, often undermine our own potential.

But boys and men also fall short of their dreams. Maybe a young man can't imagine winning a scholarship because he's the first in his family to attend college. Maybe he doesn't have experience with goal-setting. Maybe he's just shy. All of us seem to need this sort of permission: Go ahead and grab the trophy.

Honora Dent, a Washington, D.C. registered nurse, says, "I want to be the best nurse. I don't think there's anything wrong with that, because I want to take care of my patients the best possible way. I learn from the other nurses, ask them how they do things well. I take into account my limitations, but I'm always striving to be the best that I can be. It comes with maturity. I will not feel like a loser if I'm not the best, but I think it's good to want that, to try for that. I find it energizing."

The Japanese have an adage: "The nail that sticks up will be hammered down." The saying reflects the traditional Japanese emphasis on group harmony over individual achievement and accolades. Japanese athlete Junko Tabei, the first woman to climb Mt. Everest (in 1975), now advises, "be the nail that sticks up."

"I came out here to beat everybody in sight and that's just what I'm going to do," said Babe Didrikson to the press at the 1932 Olympic trials. She kept her word, winning six gold medals and breaking four world records at those trials, single-handedly defeating the second-place team, Illinois Athletic Club, which had 22 members. Few are so brash. But when I was a child, hers was the only female-athlete biography I could find in the elementary school library. I read it over and over again, searching for clues as to how to be an athlete, how to win, how to be good at everything, the way Babe was.

In addition to her stunning track and field performances, Babe excelled at basketball, tennis, swimming, football, lacrosse, bowling, fencing, skating, shooting, billiards, cycling, and baseball. She struck out Joe Dimaggio. She co-founded the LPGA, won 17 golf tournaments in a row — and played a mean harmonica. She once bragged to a roommate that she was really good at ironing. Why aren't more of us that committed to excellence?

Try saying this: I want to win. Try saying to a friend: I want to be as good as you at surfing or parenting or selling tires. You might feel terribly vulnerable. What if you fail? What if your friend feels threatened by your ambition? Here's why it can be worth taking that risk: When you're honest about what you want, you open up the possibility of success — and intimacy. You allow others to see who you are, and you allow the light of day to shine on your ambitions. Then they won't seem shameful and secretive. There's nothing wrong with wanting to win.

It's in that striving, and in that willingness to try hard, that you find out not only what you can do, but who you are.

C. Lynn Centonze, Chief of Police in Fairfield, New Jersey, played field hockey and lacrosse in high school and college (West Chester State), and says she still visits her high school field hockey coach, Linda Alimi of West Essex High School in North Caldwell, New Jersey, "to thank her for what she taught me."

The biggest lesson? "Losing is not an option," says Centonze. "Don't get defeated before you start. Whatever your competition or engagement is for that day, all energy goes toward success, not fear of losing, which is paralyzing. I used this as a road officer, where you have to make the right decisions in order to stay out of harm's way. Now, as an administrator, I have to win on behalf of my officers. I'm not shy about stating what I know to be correct, or what we need to get the job done. I know it's okay to be a strong female, and to hold your own."

Inspired by Pete Sampras's famous U.S. Open match in which he won despite vomiting on the court, Centonze says her motto is, "Never give up. When you're out there on the streets doing good things for people, you've got to believe you can win, and you've got to keep fighting."

Process and results both matter

In the American culture, it's obvious that winning matters. "You have to win," tennis pioneer Billie Jean King has said. "Otherwise, no one pays any attention to what you say."

It's harder to remember that process matters, too. Corporate, academic, and athletic "winners" are easily forgiven for rudeness and other "minor" transgressions — as long as they win. But in fact, winning and how you win both matter. If the result is not good — if you wanted very much to win, and didn't — you will be disappointed. You might also lose out on tangible rewards offered to the winner. But if the process is not good — if you cheat, if the other person cheats, if you are insufficiently challenged, or if for any reason you do not enjoy the actual play or work — the victory will be tainted, dull, or meaningless.

Balance is essential. Too much focus on the result will lead to a sloppy or unethical process. And too much focus on the process will yield an unsatisfying result.

> Winning is a nice thing that happens on the way toward achieving your goals.
>
> — Susan Bassett, athletic director, William Smith College

Are there competitive situations in which process is not important? At Wimbledon, for instance, are the players focused only on victory? If so, they won't win. During a competitive event, successful elite athletes focus on hitting a ball, getting to the right court position, and responding to the opposition. They're aware of the score, but they're also aware of what's happening on the court — and in their bodies — during each moment of play. It's when athletes focus only on the end result that they injure themselves. Or they injure their integrity through cheating. Or they injure other players through recklessness. They injure their chances of success.

Destroying one's own body or others' bodies in the name of victory is a pervasive athletic model in American society. (See "Q is for Quitting.") Some respond by saying we should not keep score — that winning itself is at fault. I'm suggesting that there is an alternative approach. We can strive for victory and create a respectful process at the same time. We can be both competitive and compassionate. It's possible to focus on the self and the other at the same time. It's possible to focus on both the goal and the means to achieve that goal.

The difference between trying to win and just doing your best

"I'm not trying to win," people tell me. "I'm just doing my best."

I wonder: Why not do both?

"Coach Wooden taught us that doing the best you are capable of is victory enough," said Kareem Abdul-Jabaar. But Coach Wooden, whose UCLA teams won a record ten national championships, also taught Kareem and his teammates how to win. He taught them to expect to win. And he taught them to be gracious in victory, as he himself always was. He found that elusive balance between understanding just how important winning is and just how unimportant it is.

"Just do your best" is a popular parental suggestion, and one that can relieve pressure that probably doesn't belong on small children in the first place. It conveys a message of unconditional love, regardless of whether a child wins or loses.

But the word "just" suggests that what's called for is a limited effort. It also avoids any comparison with others, a philosophical position that overlooks the joys and benefits of competition. Consider the difference between "Just do your best" and "I think you can win." Which one makes the heart race with excitement and anticipation? Which is a more affirming message to give a child?

"I think you can win" not only conveys confidence, it puts forth a specific goal and calls forth courage, because the person who tries to win must also be prepared to face defeat. The stakes are much higher than "just do your best," and in general, when stakes are raised, attention becomes more focused and achievement improves.

When you dare to seek victory, your reward comes not so much with the trophy, prize money, or bragging rights, but with the test itself, the sense of rising to the challenge and discovering what's good and strong in yourself. There must be a goal. And you have to care. You can't say (as many nonathletic women do), "Let's not keep score." If you don't keep score, you won't "try hard," and if you don't try hard, you won't find out what you can do. Winning is a carrot to entice you to try harder — not because of what happens to you if you win, but because of what happens to you if you try.

I also hear, "All you can do is your best." That's not true. You can do more. You can do your best *to win*, which is different. "Do your best" lets you off the hook. Striving to be the best is a higher goal.

On the other hand, winning is not necessarily the wisest goal, either — if it's unrealistic, or if it's too easy. Susan Bassett, athletic director at William Smith College in Geneva, New York, presides over a program that has won four national championships (one in soccer, three in field hockey) since 1988. Their basketball team has won more than 90 percent of their games in the past 13 years. The other teams are similarly stellar.

Bassett says, "We win so much that we can fool ourselves, and get satisfied too early. I don't want us to feel we're 'there yet,' because ultimately what we want to do is reach our potential. So I tell my athletes and coaches, 'Winning is a nice thing that happens on the way toward achieving your goals.'

"To get the most out of an experience, you have to see what you can do, see how much knowledge you can acquire, see how good you can feel about yourself," says Bassett. "It's all about achieving excellence. Winning is one way to measure that, but it's not the only way."

The risk of failure

If you admit you want to win, you become accountable for your eventual success or failure. Whereas if you never admit you want to win, you can always hang out in the back of the pack with the folks who claim, "I wasn't really trying to win. I'm just here to have fun."

In fact, failure can be a great teacher. "It's probably good for me to lose," said Venus Williams after losing to Martina Hingis in the 1999 French Open quarterfinals. "When you're winning, you aren't always able to see the things you are doing wrong. I guess you have horse blinders on a bit. Now I'm able to see."

Here's some more advice for athletes:

- Define victory for yourself. You're the one who should decide if learning to ski the bunny slope, or finishing one year of college, qualifies as a victory. Don't let anyone else impose their definition on you.

- If, during a competition, it becomes apparent that you can't win, change your definition of victory so you can have something new to strive for.

- Hang out with winners. Observe their behavior and their attitude. Learn everything you can from them, including how *not* to act.

- Watch sports — not to root for the home team, but to see how college and professional athletes behave in pursuit of victory. Decide which ones you want to emulate.

- After you win, shake hands. After you lose, shake hands.

- After you lose, console yourself by reminding yourself of all the good things you did — took risks, challenged yourself, developed strength or competence, tried new things. Be kind to yourself, the way you would to anyone else who tried and failed.

- Keep perspective. Even football legend Vince Lombardi, credited with the infamous line, "Winning isn't everything, it's the only thing," didn't really mean that, according to James Michener in *Sport in America*. Lombardi retracted the statement shortly before he died. "I wish to hell I'd never said that damn thing," he told Jerry Izenberg. "I meant the effort... I meant having a goal...I sure as hell didn't mean for people to crush human values and morality."

- To get competitive experience in a safe setting, challenge people to simple, playful games, like shooting paper wads into a trash can or dueling with empty wrapping-paper rolls. Notice how you feel when you win or lose. Joke with your friends and colleagues about who's going to win in minor competitions at work and at home. Practice saying, "I'm going to win." Play Ping-Pong, bowling, bridge, hearts, or Scrabble, and keep score. Try to win. See if you get tense about it, or overly disappointed at loss. Use every game as a mirror to see yourself better.

W is for Winning: Give yourself permission to be the best.

* * * * *

TIME OUT FOR REFLECTION

1) What, if anything, keeps you from winning as much or as often as you could?

_____

_____

2) If absolutely nothing got in your way, what would you attempt to win?

_____

_____

3) Judging from your actions, which is more important to you, process or results? Explain.

_____

_____

4) Considering your current challenges, how would you define victory?

_____

_____

X is for eXpectations

A birdie on every hole

X is for eXpectation
How far can you see?
What's blocking your vision
Of all you could be?

On October 22, 1988, Paula Newby-Fraser, a 26-year-old South African triathlete, ran from the shores of Hawaii's Kona Coast into the Pacific Ocean and promptly became anonymous: a red-capped sardine flailing her muscular arms and legs partly for locomotion, partly for self-defense. When she emerged, dripping, almost an hour later, most of the other 1,274 swimmers were still thrashing through the waves.

Paula ran to the transition station to find her bike. She had just completed the first third of the Ironman, the grueling race that began as a beer-inspired bet in 1978 and gave birth to the word "triathlon." Fifteen men had entered that first swim-bike-run competition. By 1988, a decade later, the Bud Light Ironman Triathlon World Championship had ballooned into a televised event offering $150,000 in prize money to the top 15 male and 10 female finishers in an international field of 1,275, including 240 women. Paula Newby-Fraser had won this race before, in 1986.

As happens in road races, female and male Ironmen begin at the same time and cover the same distance, in this case a 2.4-mile ocean swim, a 112-mile bike ride through hilly lava fields, and finally a marathon — a 26.2-mile run, walk, or stumble, depending on one's condition. The best men finish first, so to say Paula has won is to say she has won *the women's division* of the race.

The best Ironwoman had, until 1988, always finished more than an hour behind the best man. In 1987, the female winner placed 26th overall. Which is why Paula Newby-Fraser's 11th place overall finish in 1988 shocked the triathlon community — and Paula herself — and upset long-established notions of what women can do.

> "You're much better than they are," she told me. "You should be eating them up out there."

During the bike ride Paula gained momentum, pedaling past each of the four women who had outswum her, including Erin Baker, the record-holder from New Zealand. Paula didn't know how fast she was going. She had a watch on, but she didn't look at it because she didn't want to feel hurried. "I felt happy enough that if I blew up at the Ironman, that was too bad," she said. "I had a very relaxed mental attitude."

Paula relaxed through the marathon run as well. The route has an out-and-back layout, and as she approached the turnaround point, she saw her boyfriend, Paul Huddle, running at a slower pace. She had never before passed him in a race, and had never dreamed that she would. "It's terrible," she says, "but I didn't want to pass him. When I saw him, I'm going, 'No, that's not him.' When I got closer, I'm going, 'Oh my god, it's him.'"

Paul Huddle had finished 15th in the 1987 Ironman. Paula passed him without so much as a nod. "I didn't know what to say," she explains in a still-strong South African accent. "I want Paul to excel in his chosen sport as much as I want to do well. I didn't realize at the time that he was doing well." She was thinking, If I'm passing him, he must be having a terrible day.

He was having a fine day. He eventually finished 15th among the men again — 16th overall, because of Paula's 11th place overall finish. "Good job, keep it going, you look really strong," he called as Paula, six inches shorter and sixty pounds lighter, sped past.

Chris Hinshaw, a friend of Paul's, was near them at the time. "Let's go with her," he suggested to Paul.

"*You* go with her," Paul gasped. "She was moving twenty seconds a mile faster than us at the time," he explains. "I would have exploded if I tried to go with her. At that point in the race, you just want to finish. But a lot of guys were in shock."

Some teased Paul. "She's in front of you, she's beating you," they taunted.

"Shut up, she's beating you too," came his reply.

Paula crossed the finish line with enough energy left over for a triumphant raised-arms salute, having sliced more than half an hour — 34 minutes and 24 seconds — off the women's record. She finished a mere 12 seconds after the 10th-place man and just thirty minutes and one second after the male winner, Scott Molina. Her time of 9:01:01 would have been fast enough to beat all of the men in any of the Ironman triathlons before 1984.

"I never thought a woman could go this fast," she said.

Now, she knew that, from the men's times in the previous four years, a *person* could go that fast. She knew that, in a sport merely ten years old, improvement was inevitable. Nevertheless, she had developed in her mind a limit on female performance — and hence on her own capacity for success.

Paula's comment — "I never thought a woman could go this fast" — has implications for women's performance relative to men's. It also illustrates a general human tendency to limit ourselves with ideas about what we — or people like us — might achieve. Some people don't think a person without formal education can teach. Some don't think a refugee can open a successful business. Some don't think an amputee can be an athlete. We don't believe we ourselves can be athletes, or actors, or astronauts, or accountants, because we lack the _____. What is it we lack, and do we really lack it? And is it really necessary to achieve our goals? Sometimes all we lack is an *expectation* of success, a belief in our own ability to succeed.

Eating them up out there

Sometimes expectations can be altered by a trusted authority figure. My Stanford coaches did this for me — helped me expect more of myself. I remember one time in particular. We were losing to "Sac State," (now the University of California at Sacramento). My teammates and I were shooting baskets during the halftime break, trying to stay loose, trying to re-focus on what we needed to do to win the game.

Sue Rojcewicz, our assistant coach, took me aside. Sue had played on the 1976 Olympic team, and she scrimmaged with us sometimes in practice, exhibiting a wild-armed intensity I'd never before witnessed up close. While the rest of us jogged through drills, Sue sprinted, lunging for loose balls and grabbing rebounds with the ferocity of a starving animal. Every pass was a potential steal, every rebound was hers, every moment she was fully alert, fully involved, and fully committed to all-out excellence. I had tremendous respect for her.

"You're much better than they are," she told me. "You should be eating them up out there."

"Uh, me?" I wanted to ask. I was surprised. I had never really thought of what I "should" be doing; I had just played. Truth is, I was already the best player in the region, and had awards to prove it. I was already dominating most games, leading in scoring and rebounding. But I must have been having a lackluster performance that day, and Sue was telling me what she expected of me: I should be "eating them up." Her colorful language struck me as wonderfully, aggressively competitive; it appealed to the part of me that has always been a little too nice, too ready to please. She was reminding me that I was the most talented player on the floor, and she was insisting that I should show it. I remember thinking, "Oh, yes, I suppose she's right."

When I returned to the game, I played as if desperate to claim each rebound, as if sure all my shots to go in, as if no one should dare shoot over me, or I'd swipe the ball away with my big paw. It worked — we did win the game — and more importantly,

Sue's advice became a mantra for me, and changed my expectations of myself. Before every game, I said to myself with a smile, "You should be eating them up out there," and before every practice, I reminded myself to play with my whole heart and soul, as Sue did. Her advice, her example, and her confidence in me have stayed with me. I still give myself Sue's pep talk when I find myself in a new or uncomfortable situation: "Mariah, you're very good at this. You should be eating them up out there."

Twelve years after I graduated, Stanford won its first national championship in basketball. By then, Tara VanDerveer was the coach. She knew her team had the talent to win it all, but never having won before, the players didn't really know that they could. They didn't really *expect* to.

VanDerveer consulted Stanford swimming coach Richard Quick, whose team had already won two national titles. His advice: "The players have to get comfortable with the idea of being national champs," he said.

VanDerveer posted a sign on the locker room door: "1990 National Champions: Get Comfortable With It."

"It stayed on the door all year," recalls VanDerveer. "Some people said, 'Isn't that cocky? With the opposing teams walking by and seeing it?' I said, 'No, it's just our goal.'" The team won the championship. Two years later they won again. They haven't won since — getting comfortable with the prospect of success is only one requirement for success — but it's an important one.

> The world is full of perceived limitations that stop us from being as good as we really are.
>
> — Swedish National Golf Team Coach Pia Nilsson

The 54 vision

In golf, there's an expression: "There's always hope on the first tee." It's a winking acknowledgment of why golfers return to the course again and again, even though their scores often fail to match their dreams. Regardless of how you did yesterday, you hope to do better today.

Pia Nilsson, coach of the Swedish National Team, asks these provocative questions: What exactly are we hoping for when we approach that first tee? And how might our play change if our hopes changed?

Nilsson calls her philosophy "the 54 vision." She asks her players, including some of the LPGA's best — Annika Sorenstam, Liselotte Neumann, Helen Alfredsson — to expect a birdie on every hole, which would add up to a score of 54, not the par (usually 72) that most players use as a measuring stick.

"Par is so limiting," Nilsson says. "Par is something they came up with many hundreds of years ago. Two putts on a green was figured normal, but it doesn't need to be that. I believe it's good to have a model that is totally different, and that's what we're striving toward. On their home courses, [our players] usually make birdie on every single hole at one time or another, so each player can see herself making birdie on all eighteen holes. She just hasn't done it all in a row yet. So instead of having a goal of 'Now I'm going to be the European champion' or 'I'm going to win two US Opens within five years,' why not strive for 54 — birdie on every hole?"[1]

Like many people who have high expectations, Nilsson encounters resistance. People argue, "But then you're so disappointed every time you don't shoot fifty-four."

"They don't understand," explains Nilsson. "It doesn't have to do with that. As a coach, I've chosen to believe that the potential is there. As players, they've chosen to believe that the potential is there. It's not a mandate. It's a fun challenge. What the 54 vision says is this: Dare to go beyond the limits. The world is full of perceived limitations that stop us from being as good as we really are; 54 helps us to keep on getting better."

Of all the players in the LPGA, who has come closest to achieving this goal? Sorenstam, who in 2001 became the first woman to shoot 59 and the first woman to win more than $2 million.

The 54 vision asks us to change our expectations of ourselves. It's not just about aiming high, it's about expecting a lot — perhaps more than anyone has expected of a person with our background, skills, experiences.

Paula Newby-Fraser now compares herself to the best male triathletes. No longer competing against her ideas of how fast a woman can go, she asks herself, How fast can a person go? And what do I need to do to go that fast, or faster? She hasn't passed all the men in an Ironman yet, but she still holds the women's record, which she set again in 1992 (8:55:28), and she has won the race eight times. She has won more Ironman Triathlons (around the world) than any other triathlete, male or female. Mark Allen and Erin Baker have won eight each. Dave Scott has won seven. Paula Newby-Fraser has won twenty-one.

X is for eXpectations: A birdie on every hole.

* * * * *

TIME OUT FOR REFLECTION

1) Whom do you know who seems to place no limits on what they can do?

2) Who told you, early in your life, what your capabilities and limitations were? What did they tell you?

3) What do you expect of yourself now: in sports, in school, at work?

4) How might your expectations be limiting your performance?

_____

_____

5) How could you adopt a new vision of who you might become?

_____

_____

Y is for Yes I Can

Behave as if you believe in yourself

Y is for Yes.
No need to shout.
But say it out loud
To vanquish your doubt.

W e all hear two kinds of statements about ourselves: Positive, supportive, encouraging statements (the Voice of Confidence), and negative, critical, even cruel statements (the Voice of Doubt). Sometimes we hear the Voice of Confidence and the Voice of Doubt in our own inner thoughts, and sometimes we hear these voices from others.

On a recent vacation in Florida, I heard the Voice of Doubt. It was two voices, actually, both doubting me, and both coming from 50 or so yards behind me. They were male voices, and they were shouting.

I had been having a good day. I had been avoiding the sand traps as well as the ponds, where alligators would occasionally slip their snouts out of the water as if curious about our putting prowess. I had seen a bald eagle perched regally in a tall tree near the twelfth hole, and had watched as her two young eaglets practiced flying, hopping and fluttering in their humongous nest. It was a glorious day for golf.

From the red tee to the green on the par-four fourteenth hole was 214 yards. (Red tees are still sometimes called "ladies' tees," but they're actually appropriate for junior, senior, and novice men as well as most women. The white tees, farther from the hole, are for people who are stronger or very experienced, including most men and some very good women. I'm a red-tee player.)

Between the tee and the green was a stream. Katie, my partner, hit the ball about 150 yards, laying it up neatly just in front of the stream that separated the fairway from the green. For her second shot, Katie planned to hit the ball over the water and onto the green. That's what most people playing from the red tees would do.

I was planning to hit the ball the entire 214 yards — over the fairway, over the water, and, I hoped, onto the green. On a good day, I can hit it that far. So I stood at the tee, waiting for the foursome ahead of us to finish putting. I didn't want to hit them with my drive.

From somewhere behind me, I heard men yelling. I've never before been yelled at on a course (except when someone shouts, "Fore!") so it took me a while to understand what the commotion was about, and that it was directed at me. Finally, I looked around and saw two men standing at the white tees, about 50 yards behind me.

"You can't hit the ball that far!" they were yelling. "Go ahead and drive! You can't hit the ball that far!"

Without thinking, I cupped my hand to the side of my mouth and shouted back, "YES I CAN!"

That felt great — but just for about two seconds, because then I had to do it. I wasn't sure I could. I am not a great golfer. On a good day, I break 95.

But I reminded myself: I'm an athlete. I can drive a ball up to 240 yards. During an athletic lifetime, I've hit many balls with many sticks. I'm coordinated, strong, and flexible. I know how to perform under pressure. While playing in Belgrade, Yugoslavia with my French professional basketball team, I sank two overtime free throws when the game was tied and 5000 people were watching me, cheering for Yugoslavia, screaming for me to miss. I know how not to choke.

I continued to wait for the people on the green to finish putting. Katie offered encouraging words. "You can do it," she said quietly, confidently.

Finally, I addressed the ball, took a deep breath, pulled the club slowly back, then whipped it around. I heard the club hit the ball with that satisfying "ping" sound that Ping clubs are named for, then watched with delight as the tiny moon arched over the fairway, over the water, and onto the grass on the other side. It landed way off to the right, off the green, but that was okay. I had said I could, and I did.

One friend, hearing this story, speculated that he would have then turned to the men and made an obscene gesture. This did not occur to me. Any further interaction with the men would have been redundant (and I never make obscene gestures.) They had publicly doubted my ability, and I had responded. That's all there was to say.

> On my way to the top, I chanted the famous line from *The Little Engine That Could*, "I think I can, I think I can..."

Feisty and fun

But I did take pleasure in having proved myself — especially since I've met male golfers who tend to lump all women into one slow, chatty community. I took pleasure in (possibly) having proved something about women in general, or female potential. I like to believe that men who watch good female golfers (especially those who are better than I am) go home and tell their partners or daughters or sons, "I saw a woman today who can hit the heck out of the ball." I like to believe that women's public demonstrations of sports skills have a subtle effect on the belief systems of people who are a bit behind the times.

But luckily, I don't play golf for other people. I play because I enjoy trying to hit the ball farther (and straighter) today than I did yesterday. I play to have fun, and to learn how good I can get. (I confess to indulging in some wildly irrational fantasies of joining the LPGA tour.)

I also play to develop confidence and stamina and patience that I can employ beyond the sports world. So ever since that day on the golf course, I've incorporated the phrase "Yes I can!" into my beyond-sports vocabulary. It's feisty and fun.

> **Where does this come from, this willingness to say, "Yes I can?"**

When Nancy Reagan initiated her "Just say no" campaign, it seemed to me that she had it backwards. The phrase should be "Just say yes" — not to drugs, of course, but to many of the challenges that life presents to us. As motivational slogans go, "Yes I can" is even better, I think, than "Just say yes," because it implies a contradiction. Someone has said, "No you can't," and the response is, "Yes I can." It's a personal pep talk, sure to come in handy next time I'm faced with something I very much want to do, and am not sure I can do, and maybe can't do. But just maybe, "Yes I can."

As a teenager in Arizona, my friends and I used to go "tubing" in the Verde River. About a dozen of us would spend a day twirling along the river in inner tubes, connected to each other with ropes and followed by our "supply tube," filled with drinks and food. There was nothing scary about the river itself. The "rapids" meandered around a few boulders, creating little whitewater. But just beyond one bend, the river deepened, and we parked our tubes on a little beach so some of us could climb a cliff, then leap into the river.

How high was the cliff? High enough to be scary. High enough that more than once, someone climbed to the top, peered over the cliff's edge into the river below, then climbed back down. High enough that most of us settled for the spectator role. High enough that, on my way to the top, I chanted the famous line from *The Little Engine That Could*, "I think I can, I think I can..."

My heart still races at the memory of standing on the ledge of that cliff, our friends watching expectantly as I wait, worry, plan, plot, and let everyone else go first. My brother treats the mountain ridge like a runway, backing up several paces and taking a long running leap, yelling as he disappears from our view. Our friend Greg Shepherd stands on the ledge quietly, building suspense, then amazes us all with a forward flip. Finally I'm alone on the cliff, and there's nothing left to do but take a few deep breaths, summon all my courage, and force myself to leap out and away. The fast fall itself is a thrill, one moment flying downward, arms swung up above me like a collapsed umbrella, the next moment far beneath the water's surface, struggling to swim back up. Even more fun is the pride of accomplishment after I emerge exultant. "I knew I could!"

Where does this come from, this willingness to say, "Yes I can?" From experience. From practice. From habit. From a commitment to leading a life filled with risk and adventure.

A recreational "tuber" says "Yes I can," then flings her body off a cliff. An Olympic diver says, "Yes I can," then nails a reverse two-and-a-half off the high platform. A painter says, "Yes I can," then finds the creativity and stamina to complete a mural. A therapist says, "Yes I can," then summons the patience to deal with a difficult client. A researcher says, "Yes I can" find a cure. A teen says, "Yes I can" refuse to drink at this party. A former smoker says, "Yes I can" make it through another day without smoking.

That time on the golf course, the two people doubting me were just impatient strangers. Next time it might be friends or family members or colleagues or editors or readers or audience members. Or it may be the loudest, most doubting voice of all, the one inside my own head: "You can't do that, Mariah!"

Now I have an answer, and I recommend it, whether your opponents are strangers on golf courses or colleagues at work or family members who lack confidence in your abilities. They might challenge you openly, or they might just live inside your head, whispering negative thoughts. Say, "Yes, I can," especially when you're not sure if you can or not. Then give it a shot.

"We have been raised to fear the "yes" within ourselves, our deepest cravings," wrote the poet Audre Lorde.

Y is for Yes I Can: Behave as if you believe in yourself.

* * * * *

TIME OUT FOR REFLECTION

1) Who doubts your abilities? What impact has this person had on you?

_____

_____

2) When have you allowed someone else to limit your performance? What did they say that caused you to lose faith in yourself?

_____

_____

3) When have you said "Yes I can" to someone or some challenge, and what was the result?

_____

_____

4) In what current arena might "Yes I can" come in handy?

_____

_____

Z is for Zone

Run your own race

Z is for Zone
Train well so you're seeing
The whole ball and whole game
Such focus is freeing.

We've all been there. We're working with a client, we're writing a paper, we're laughing around the dinner table, we're planning a meeting, we're smacking a tennis ball, we're planting bulbs in the backyard — whatever the activity, we feel alert, relaxed, and at peace with ourselves and the world around us. Nothing extraordinary. Just a simple, satisfied awareness that all is well. Maybe the moment is fleeting; maybe it lasts an hour, a day, or more. This is what I think of as the zone.

Mihaly Csikszentmihalyi, author of several books on the subject, defines "flow" (conceding that "the zone" is synonymous) as "a state of consciousness in which one becomes totally absorbed in what one is doing, to the exclusion of all other thoughts and emotions." Focus alone is not sufficient, he says. "The mind and the body are working together effortlessly, leaving the person feeling that something special has just occurred." Flow "lifts experience from the ordinary to the optimal, and it is in those moments that we feel truly alive and in tune with what we are doing."[1]

> It is good to have an end to journey toward; but it is the journey that matters, in the end.
>
> — Ursula LeGuin

I believe we can experience the state of "flow" or "zone" more often than Csikszentmihalyi implies. In fact, I think that, with practice, the ordinary can become optimal, and the "something special" feeling can happen on a daily basis. Why shouldn't the mind and body work together effortlessly most of the time?

For me, the zone happens most mornings in the pool. For at least one stroke, sometimes one lap, and occasionally one whole mile, I'm fully aware of the beauty of my body, my stroke, the cool water around me. I can't force this to happen, but by getting up early, driving to the pool, and immersing myself in the water, I increase my chances of enjoying this pleasant sort of waking dream.

The zone is not about results. "It is good to have an end to journey toward; but it is the journey that matters, in the end," wrote science fiction author Ursula LeGuin. The zone experience is about embracing the journey. At the same time, high achievers are more likely than less ambitious people to become familiar with the zone because it's born of everyday concentration, combined with discipline.

I first heard about the zone from a "yoga tennis" teacher I studied with when I was a teenager. He instructed me to "see the whole ball" from the moment it left my opponent's racket to the time it hit my own. "Look for the seams in the ball," he taught me. "Watch it spin."

That's difficult. But that's not enough, he said. When hitting a tennis ball, you also need to be aware of your opponent's location. Is he close to the net? Is he heading toward one side of the court or the other? You need to remember your opponent's strengths and weaknesses. You need to be aware of your own body to make sure you don't strain muscles or get overheated or dehydrated. So being in the zone is not just about looking at something specific (the ball). Nor is it just about looking out of your peripheral vision (the court and the opponent). Nor is it just about looking inward, at your own body, thoughts, and emotions. You need to be aware of all of that, and the score, and more. The zone is about embracing the whole game of life, all at once.

People often think of the zone as a state of perfection, but things do not have to be perfect for you to experience the joy of total awareness. When you're in the zone, you keep listening, even when you're tired. You drive well, even when you're emotionally upset. You exhibit kindness to someone in the grocery store, even when your own problems feel overwhelming. To be in the zone is to be present to yourself, and to what's happening around you, and to thrive, regardless.

Sometimes, in sports and in life, we enter the zone through repetition. Other times we enter it when we step out of our "comfort zone" and into a new experience that forces us to wake up and see things in a new light. In either case, the zone experience is one of inner peace, and of connection with the environment, including other human beings.

Connie K. DeWitte, one of the highest ranking civilian women working for the military, is Deputy Assistant Secretary of the Navy for Safety. She's the senior safety advisor in the Navy, in charge of keeping our Navy and Marine Corps personnel safe and free of occupational illnesses. Her first day on the job was September 24, 2001. Her swearing-in ceremony took place in a Pentagon hallway while a few feet away, construction crews noisily hammered and drilled, renovating the building after the September 11 terrorist attacks. "I had a real sense of being a part of history," DeWitte says, recalling the ceremony. "I was celebrating this milestone in my career, while also aware of the enormity of was happening around me."

> For me, a successful day is one in which I'm fully engaged — with my work, with my loved ones, with my body, and with the flow of life itself.

Before accepting this job, DeWitte had spent seven years serving as Chief of Safety and Occupational Health for the Headquarters of the Army Corps of Engineers. "All of this is a new situation," DeWitte told me after about eight months in the Navy position. "The answers to my questions have not been written anywhere. There's much uncertainty. It's a new organization, new people, and a new role. I'm figuring out the culture, the work, the job."

While some would find this daunting, DeWitte embraces the uncertainty. "I'm just in awe of my life as it's unfolding, as I'm receiving it," she says. "Some days are incredibly challenging, but on the other hand, I feel very free and expansive. Each week is an entirely new journey."

Listen to those words: "awe, receiving, challenging, free, expansive, journey." This is the perspective of someone in the zone.

DeWitte, who thinks of herself as an athlete, says her experiences with aerobics and dance have given her the physical conditioning and mental edge she needs to handle the job. "When you are an athlete, you have the confidence to face these challenges," she says. "You say, 'I can do that.'"

Friends have assured her that within about a year, she'll feel familiar with the job — which sounds appealing. But she's also enjoying this experience. "I'm not in my comfort zone. But even when I don't know what's going on, I still know who I am. I have an okay-ness with what life is. I'm in touch with it, going into it, flowing with it."

DeWitte's leadership approach is rooted in this same acceptance zone. "There's a specialness in each person. You look at them, and you sense who they are. Then you relate synergistically. Whether you're putting together a conference or planning a presentation, you practice together. You use what everyone brings to the table. If there's a problem, you each contribute to the solution, and you create a result that's better than anyone could have done alone."

> **You are an athlete.
> Life's a game. Enjoy.**

This process reminds her, she says, of high school cheerleading, when she and her teammates would "practice our routines, work hard, and make something special together. You complement each other. That joy is very similar on the job."

When you're in the zone, challenges that might in the past have become major roadblocks are reduced to minor obstacles.

"Just last week," DeWitte confides, "I got a hard feeling over something. But now when that happens, I can tune into it. I know what to do, who to talk to, and how to talk to them. I move past it very quickly."

A delicious reward for an athletic approach to life, the zone experience reflects a mature acceptance of, and simultaneous celebration of, the way life is. It can't be forced. But can it be cultivated? Sure. How? By embracing the first twenty-five athletic essentials. See yourself as an athlete (A is for Athlete), prepare to win on an off day (B Game), welcome challenges and rise to the occasion (Competitive Spirit), develop the habit of greatness (Discipline), master the Power/Rest cycle (Endurance)... can you see how they begin to add up?

The zone is primarily about focus and intent. Do you choose to see life as "a daring adventure," as Helen Keller advised? Can you summon "awe" for your "life as it's unfolding," as Connie DeWitte does?

Martin, the triathlete and finance manager, reports, "The other day, I was assigned a project that a colleague really wanted. My assistant and I were working on it, and that other colleague kept doing everything he could to undermine us. He openly challenged our competence. My assistant was flustered and intimidated. So before a big presentation we had to make, I said to her, 'Just run your own race. Don't think about where he is, or what he's doing. That will only throw you off-balance. Just run your own race.' And she aced it."

People define success in various ways. I encourage you to define it for yourself. For me, a successful day is one in which I'm fully engaged — with my work, with my loved ones, with my body, and with the flow of life itself. I'm running my own race. For me, success is not about controlling my environment, making everything turn out the way I want it to. The magic of goal-setting and the importance of tangible accomplishments notwithstanding, life just can't be manipulated like that.

"My definition of comfort has changed," explains DeWitte. "It used to be that I needed predictability. Now I don't. The circumstances change, but I have strong sense of myself, and there's a deep comfort in that."

Her job — and her life — remind her of whitewater rafting, DeWitte says. "You're going on a trip and enjoying it. You don't know what's ahead. You do certain things to prepare and protect yourself, like hire a guide who knows the river. But you're not sure what happens next. You go into that flow with a lot of confidence and faith. Not only is it okay, it's great fun."

You are an athlete. Life is a game. Enjoy.

Z is for Zone: Run your own race.

* * * * *

Time Out for Reflection

1) When's the last time you had a feeling of being in the zone?

_____

_____

2) How would you describe your physical and mental state when you're in the zone?

_____

_____

3) What circumstances seem to lead you toward that feeling of rightness with yourself and the world around you?

_____

_____

Acknowledgments

I'm indebted to author and friend Sam Horn, who understood this book immediately, came up with the title and other key concepts, edited the manuscript, and offered wonderful support and enthusiasm. (S is for Sam!)

Thanks to Barbara Feinman and Sue Schaffer for carefully reading the manuscript and giving me extremely useful feedback.

Thanks to Susan Devereaux, my marvelous assistant, for helping with research on this book and keeping my career on track in numerous ways.

Thanks to Felicia Eth, my longtime agent, who offered her usual honest and helpful advice and perspective.

Thanks to all the people I interviewed. I appreciate your time and your thoughtfulness. Thanks especially to Donna Lopiano and Linda Bunker for early input on the book concept.

Thanks to Coach John Flanagan, all my swimming and golfing pals, chiropractor Bill Booker, and chiropractic assistant George Obando for helping me practice what I preach.

I'm grateful to the Poetry Grrrls (Jen Daniels, Katherine Gekker, Martha Kreiner, Michelle Mandolia, Alexander Traugott, and Katherine J. Williams), who fill our home with laughter, good food, and good writing.

Thanks also to my speaking mastermind group (Ron Culberson, Rick Maurer, Arnie Sanow, Lynne Waymon), my women's mastermind group (Margaret Anderson, Jean Stafford, and Pat Woolsey) and my Awesome Authors group (Maggie Bedrosian, Barbara Feinman, Sam Horn, and Lynne Waymon) for all your wise ideas, gentle suggestions, and affectionate humor.

Thanks to my many friends for being who you are. I love you dearly.

And thanks to my Zen guide, Cheri Huber.

Last but not least, I would like to thank parents, Sarah and Art, and my siblings, Carol and Peter, who have long shared with me their love of language, sports, reading, writing, and public speaking. Thanks especially to Mom and Pete for being good sports when they keep showing up as characters in the play of my life. Heartfelt thanks to all my family members, including cousins, aunts, uncles, and steps, but especially Katherine, Bernie, Linda, Tom, Carolyn, Kate, Chris, Suzanne, and all the "niblings": Teagan, Alex, Annaliese, Chrissie, Lianna, Jason, Willow Mariah, and Baby X. And thanks to Rocky for modeling unconditional love (to err is human, to forgive, canine.)

Notes

E is for Endurance

1 Wayne Muller, *Sabbath: Restoring the Sacred Rhythm of Rest* (New York: Bantam Books, 1999), p. 5.

2 Muller, p. 30.

F is for Forgiveness

1 Atul Gawande, *Complications: A Surgeon's Notes on an Imperfect Science* (New York: Metropolitan Books, 2002).

H is for Humility

1 For more information about the National Speakers Association, call 480/968-2552 or go to www.NSASpeaker.org.

K is for Knowledge

1 Brian Reid, "The Nocebo Effect: Placebo's Evil Twin," *Washington Post* (April 30, 2002,) p. F1.

L is for Leadership

1 See Lolma Olson's website, www.sageteam.com, for more information.

M is for Mental Game

1 Shari Young Kuchenbecker, *Raising Winners: A Parent's Guide to Helping Players Succeed On and Off the Field* (New York: Random House, 2000).

P is for Purpose

1 Thanks to Lauren Crux for this definition.

2 Verbs are from Laurie Beth Jones' book, *The Path: Creating Your Mission Statement for Work and for Life* (New York: Hyperion, 1996).

R is for Rebound

1 Frances Willard, *A Wheel Within a Wheel: How I Learned to Ride the Bicycle: With Some Reflections by the Way* (Bedford, MA: Applewood Books, 1997, republished from Fleming H. Revell Company, 1895), p. 22.

2 Willard, p. 26.

3 Antonio Machado, "Last Night as I was Sleeping," translation by Robert Bly, in Roger Housden, *Ten Poems to Change Your Life*, (New York: Harmony Books, 2002), p. 21.

S is for Strong

1 "Beyond 50: A Report to the Nation on Trends in Health Security," AARP (www.aarp.org), May 21, 2002.

2 Sally Squires, "In It for the Long Run," *Washington Post* (April 23, 2002), p. F3.

T is for Teamwork

1 Peter Perl, "Hallowed Ground," *Washington Post Magazine* (May 12, 2002), p. 35.

2 Michael Silver, "Papa Bear," *Sports Illustrated* (May 6, 2002), p. 56.

3 Christine Brennan, "Honoring Brother, Today and Beyond," *USA Today* (October 11, 2001), p. C3.

4 For more information on Jeremy's Heroes, go to www.JeremysHeroes.com.

5 Jim Collins, "Good to Great," *Fast Company* (October 2001), pp. 92, 100.

X is for eXpectations

1 Mona Vold, *Different Strokes* (New York: Simon & Schuster 1999), p. 221.

Z is for Zone

1 Susan A. Jackson and Mihaly Csikszentmihalyi, *Flow in Sports: The Keys to Optimal Experiences and Performances* (Champaign, Ill: Human Kinetics, 1999), p. 5.

Index

About the Author

A Stanford University basketball player ('78; one rebounding record remains unbroken,) Mariah Burton Nelson, M.P.H., played for a pro team in France and in the first women's pro basketball league in the United States (the WBL).

The author of four other ground-breaking books, Mariah writes for *Newsweek*, the *Washington Post*, the *New York Times*, *USA Today*, *Fitness*, *Glamour*, *Cosmopolitan*, *Redbook*, and other publications, and appears on *Today*, *Good Morning America*, *Dateline*, *Crossfire*, *Larry King Live*, *PrimeTime Live*, *National Public Radio*, *HBO*, *ESPN*, etc.

Past President of the National Speakers Association/ Washington, D.C., Nelson has been giving customized keynotes since 1987. Known for her originality and humor, Nelson uses her 26 athletic essentials, business research, audience participation, and video to show people how to lead and succeed with courage, compassion, commitment, and confidence. Clients include corporations (Accenture, Brim Healthcare, IBM, Fairview Health Services, Merrill Lynch), associations (American Organization of Nurse Executives, National Association of Secondary School Principals, Young Presidents Organization), government groups (U.S. Navy, U.S. Department of Justice, General Services Administration), and colleges (Smith, Colgate, Ohio State), plus hundreds of others.

Committed to practicing what she preaches, she swims two miles most mornings, drives golf balls up to 240 yards, and applies athletic essentials such as discipline, integrity, teamwork, leadership, and joy to her career as an author, journalist, and speaker. She also coaches her mother, Sarah, who holds two Arizona State breaststroke records for women aged 75-79.

Mariah lives in Arlington, Virginia.

Contact Information

To find out more about Mariah Burton Nelson's
speeches or writing, contact Mariah

c/o Dare Press
2909 North 24th Street
Arlington, VA 22207

703-276-8323

www.MariahBurtonNelson.com

WAAA@MariahBurtonNelson.com

For individual or bulk orders: 888-281-5170